WILLIAMSON

EMILY STEAD

ULTIMATE FOOTBALL HEROES

WILLIAMSON

FROM THE PLAYGROUND
TO THE PITCH

First published by Dino Books in 2023,
an imprint of Bonnier Books UK,
4th Floor, Victoria House, Bloomsbury Square, London WC1B 4DA
Owned by Bonnier Books,
Sveavägen 56, Stockholm, Sweden

@UFHbooks
@footieheroesbks
www.heroesfootball.com
www.bonnierbooks.co.uk

Design by www.envydesign.co.uk

Paperback ISBN: 978 1 80078 637 0
E-book ISBN: 978 1 78946 717 8

British Library cataloguing-in-publication data:
A catalogue record for this book is available from the British Library.

Printed and bound in Great Britain by Clays Ltd, Elcograf S.p.A.

1 3 5 7 9 10 8 6 4 2

For captains everywhere –

lead like Leah.

ULTIMATE FOOTBALL HEROES

Emily Stead has loved writing for children ever since she was a child herself! Working as a children's writer and editor, she has created books about some of football's biggest stars, teams and tournaments for many a season. She remains a passionate supporter of women's football and Leeds United.

Cover illustration by Dan Leydon.
To learn more about Dan, visit danleydon.com
To purchase his artwork visit etsy.com/shop/footynews
Or just follow him on Twitter @danleydon

TABLE OF CONTENTS

ACKNOWLEDGEMENTS 9

CHAPTER 1 – **FINAL SCORE** 11

CHAPTER 2 – **GUNNERS VERSUS SPURS** 18

CHAPTER 3 – **HIGHBURY HAPPINESS** 25

CHAPTER 4 – **A YOUNG GUNNER** 31

CHAPTER 5 – **VERY IMPORTANT VISITORS** 38

CHAPTER 6 – **SCOUTED BY ENGLAND** 45

CHAPTER 7 – **ONE OF OUR OWN** 51

CHAPTER 8 – **NERVES OF STEEL** 58

CHAPTER 9 – **BATTLING BACK** 65

CHAPTER 10 – **WEMBLEY AWAITS** 70

CHAPTER 11 – **NORDIC CHAMPIONS** 77

CHAPTER 12 – **A LIONESS'S LEAP** 82

CHAPTER 13 – **TOP OF THE LEAGUE** 89

CHAPTER 14 – **2019 WORLD CUP** 96

CHAPTER 15 – **LESSON LEARNED** 103

CHAPTER 16 – **NOISY NEIGHBOURS** 109

CHAPTER 17 – **AN OLYMPIC DREAM** 115

CHAPTER 18 – **CAPTAIN MATERIAL** 122

CHAPTER 19 – **THE ARNOLD CLARK CUP** 129

CHAPTER 20 – **LEADING THE LIONESSES** 136

CHAPTER 21 – **THAT FINAL** 143

CHAPTER 22 – **THE EUROS EFFECT** 147

CHAPTER 23 – **WORLD CUP HEARTACHE** 152

LEAH WILLIAMSON HONOURS 159

GREATEST MOMENTS 161

TEST YOUR KNOWLEDGE 164

PLAY LIKE YOUR HEROES 166

ACKNOWLEDGEMENTS

My first thank you is to Bonnier Books UK for adding me to their *Ultimate Football Heroes* squad, for this new title in a series of books that continues to thrill young readers and football fans in their millions.

To every teacher, bookseller and librarian who has helped get the books into the hands of readers special thanks are due. And of course, an extra-special mention goes to you, the readers and fans – without you there wouldn't be any Heroes.

It is a privilege to be able to share the story of England captain and homegrown Arsenal hero, Leah Williamson. Alongside her team of fearless Lionesses, Leah continues to inspire a generation of young footballers to follow their dreams.

Long before these latest Lionesses first kicked a ball though, generations of talented women helped pave the way for women's football to grow into the game it has become today. Women like Lily Parr and Bella Reay who sadly never had the opportunity to play for an official England team, despite their lionhearted love of the game. Or Sylvia Gore and Sheila Parker who played in the first England match to be recognised by the Football Association, as late as 1972. And all the women who have since juggled studies, jobs and families, while entertaining crowds for little reward or, at times, none at all.

The fifty-year ban by the FA on women's football that so cruelly and unfairly affected generations of women and girls has meant that the game is today still playing catch-up to where it should rightfully be. But with our current squad of Lionesses who are still fighting to give *all* young people the same opportunities to enjoy the beautiful game, women's football is in the best hands. Lionesses, your legacy as champions is set to go far beyond your achievements on the pitch. Thank you.

CHAPTER 1

FINAL SCORE

31 July 2022, London
Women's Euro 2022 Final – England vs Germany

As Leah led her team of Lionesses onto the pitch, her usual game-face had been relegated to the dressing room. She was so happy to be at Wembley Stadium on this momentous day, she couldn't help but smile. The team had worked so hard to get to this final, winning every match on their way. Now England were ready to write a new chapter in women's football history, but first they'd have to defeat old enemies Germany.

A record crowd of 87,192 had packed into Wembley, with most of those supporting the

Lionesses. When the stadium announcer read out the teams, the fans cheered wildly. Every stand in the stadium was bouncing.

'Let's do our jobs girls, but let's enjoy every minute,' Leah told her teammates in the huddle. 'An occasion like this may never come around again.'

A few seconds more and the game would kick off. Leah looked down at her captain's armband, the same rainbow armband she had worn all tournament. She was skippering England at a Euros final on home soil. *This has to be a dream, doesn't it?* she wondered. *I'm going to wake up any minute now.*

The action got underway, with both teams creating early chances. England's best opportunities had fallen to Ellen White and Lucy Bronze, but they hadn't managed to get the ball over the line.

Then after twenty-seven minutes, it was England's goal that was suddenly under attack. In a goalmouth scramble, the ball bounced up and hit Leah on the shoulder. She didn't have her arms down like the rules said she was supposed to, so the game stopped for VAR to take a look. Was it a handball? It had happened in an instant; there was nothing Leah could have done, but penalties had been given for less. Time seemed to slow to a crawl while the check was completed. If VAR gave the penalty, Leah could go from hero to villain in the blink of an eye.

When the ref blew her whistle to play on at last, Leah breathed an enormous sigh of relief. Years ago, she wouldn't have been able to move past something like this, but now the England captain knew that dwelling on a mistake would get her nowhere. Instead, she stayed positive and carried on trying to help her team.

At half-time, 0–0 was a fair scoreline. Both sides had had moments of looking dangerous, but no one had managed to break through their defences. Whoever scored first would have to produce something special.

Soon after the break, Germany's Lina Magull fired a warning shot, but the ball pinged just wide of the post. Leah was calm but she could feel a nervous energy beginning to build around the stadium. England manager Sarina Wiegman responded by making a decisive double substitution, taking off experienced goalscorers Fran Kirby and Ellen While. Leah clapped their replacements Ella Toone and Alessia Russo onto the pitch, both of them fearless young Lionesses ready to give England their all.

Not long after, injury struck. England's top scorer of the tournament, Beth Mead, went down in a fifty-fifty tackle and couldn't carry on. Chloe Kelly replaced her.

'Stay positive,' Leah cried. 'Anyone on this pitch is capable of grabbing a goal.'

Then came a chance for England, as Keira Walsh picked out Ella with an outrageous defence-splitting pass. Ella was through on goal with just the keeper to beat. And without a flicker, the super sub scooped the ball high over German keeper Merle Frohms.

Goooooooooaaaaaaaaaaaallllllllll!

'The goalscorer for England, Number 20, ELLA TOOOOOOONE!'

The cheers were so loud, they nearly lifted the Wembley roof off, arch and all!

Now 1–0 up, England had to settle quickly. With half an hour still to play, they were far from home and dry. Minutes later Germany rattled the England crossbar, before keeper Mary Earps gratefully swallowed up the rebound. Germany couldn't come much closer than that without scoring.

At last, in the seventy-ninth minute, the visitors' efforts were rewarded when forward Lina Magull equalised.

'We go again,' Leah rallied the England team. This match was far from over. In fact, if the scores stayed the same, thirty more minutes of extra time would be played.

Please not penalties, the thought flashed through Leah's mind.

But penalties weren't needed, because with just ten minutes to go, Chloe stuck a boot out to prod the ball past Frohms. Was it offside? Definitely not! 2–1 to England! The substitute took off her shirt in sheer delight and began swinging it around her head like a lasso. A yellow card was shown for the celebration, but nothing could bring Chloe down from cloud nine!

Now just minutes remained to defend a lead more precious than the Crown Jewels; England were not about to give up that lead again. Lucy and Ella held onto the ball, dragging it out to the corner flags, while Chloe's dancing feet drew fouls. With each minute that passed, Germany became more frustrated. England, though, were untouchable.

Finally, the referee's whistle blew.

ENGLAND WERE EUROPEAN CHAMPIONS!!!

And on that whistle, Leah's legs seemed to fail her. She dropped to the ground, as goosebumps spiked all over her body. It wasn't a bad sensation, far from it. She wished she could have bottled that feeling.

Millie Bright came over to help her up.

'What have we done here?' Leah hugged her, captain to vice-captain.

'Just incredible!' Millie struggled to reply.

But before Leah could start the celebrations properly, she headed to the centre circle. Sitting on the pitch was Lena Oberdorf, one hand covering her tear-stained face. The gifted young German had run Leah ragged all match, and it was only right to show her respect. The two shared a hug and a smile before England's captain joined her team.

Then without warning, Leah's own happy tears began to flow and flow. Out came every emotion she had been storing up for weeks now: joy, pride, sheer relief, but most of all love.

Six-year-old Leah, who fell in love with football at first sight, could never in her wildest dreams have imagined a day like today. This was the stuff of fairy tales.

CHAPTER 2

GUNNERS VERSUS SPURS

March 1997, Newport Pagnell, Buckinghamshire

In the cosy lounge of the Williamson family home in Newport Pagnell, Amanda and Grandma Berny sat on one sofa, with David on the other.

A couple of days earlier, proud parents Amanda and David had welcomed their first child into the world: Leah Cathrine Williamson.

Baby Leah was now sleeping soundly on her mum's chest, while the family opened presents from well-wishers.

'She's a little beauty,' said Amanda's mum, Leah's Grandma Berny, stroking the back of the baby's head.

'Isn't she just,' Amanda agreed.

While Amanda had her hands full, Berny unwrapped a small parcel wrapped in tissue paper. Inside, was a tiny red cardigan with white cuffs. Berny held it up to show Amanda and David. 'This one will really suit her,' said Berny. 'Don't you think, David?'

'Definitely not!' said Dad, opening a second package. 'This lilywhite sleepsuit is more her style.'

They were of course talking about football. Berny and Amanda were loyal Arsenal fans, while David's side of the family all supported Tottenham Hotspur. It made for some very loud times around the TV whenever the two teams faced each other in the Premier League.

'She might not even like football,' suggested Amanda, though this baby had been quite the kicker inside her tummy these past few weeks.

'I doubt that in this family,' Berny replied, with a smile.

So, would it be Highbury or White Hart Lane? Time would tell.

Leah's first love though turned out to be

gymnastics. As a tiny tot on the bars and balance beam she showed she had plenty of strength, while her floor routines were graceful. She had taken up the sport aged two, to try to correct a problem with the way she walked. By the age of five, Leah was attending classes four times a week.

Sometimes at the end of the session, the coach would roll a football across the springy floor and let the girls have a kickaround. Leah always looked forward to the mini matches – she could easily dribble around the other players and loved to shoot too. Before long, she began nagging her parents to let her play football properly.

Not every club was keen to let a girl join, but Leah's mum, Amanda, kept searching until at last she found Leah a club in nearby Bletchley and took her along for a trial. The railway line ran right alongside the pitch at Scot Youth FC, so when the trains rattled past in the middle of a match, you couldn't even hear the ref's whistle.

'It's only boys at the moment,' the coach told Amanda before Leah's first session. 'But if she's good enough, she'll play.'

Amanda was glad she had found a coach who was willing to let Leah play, but some of the boys stared at her daughter like she had three heads!

Maybe this wasn't such a good idea? Amanda worried.

She didn't tell Leah at the time, but her own experiences of playing football as a young girl were still painful to think about. She had wanted to play so badly that she'd had to cut her hair and pretend to be a boy to escape the nasty comments from opposition teams and their parents. There was no way Leah was cutting off her beautiful blonde locks!

She looked down at her daughter, little Leah, who didn't look nervous, not one bit. She already had her game-face on and ran onto the pitch with the boys without looking back.

Ten minutes later, Leah had already scored twice.

'She's good,' said a small boy with blond spiky hair. 'She can be on our team!'

After that, the boys began to pass her the ball. And before long, it was like she had always been one of the team. The boys grew to love having Leah around, especially the blond one, Mason, who became her best friend.

Still, there were those parents who thought it wasn't right that a girl could be better than their sons – but Leah played on with a smile on her face. Amanda was just glad her daughter's introduction to football was a happier one than her own.

*

It soon became clear that Leah had skills that were far beyond those of the average six-year-old boy or girl. She could do things with a football that other children couldn't master until years later.

'She's a natural,' the coach at Scot Youth told Amanda. It was music to Mum's ears! 'Have you thought about a girls' team for her?'

He told her about a girls-only academy at Rushden and Diamonds. Their fancy-sounding Centre of Excellence gave the best girls in the area the chance to play together. Leah could blossom there. It had much better pitches and proper coaches rather than parent volunteers, and so would make the forty-four-mile round trip worthwhile.

So, when she was accepted at the new academy, Leah was delighted! She would miss the boys at Scot Youth, but this was a positive step on her journey to becoming a better footballer. She knew she was lucky that her mum and dad had the time to take her to the sessions and that they had a car to get her there – many young players didn't have those luxuries.

For the next couple of seasons, the family travelled back and forth to Diamonds after school, with matches at the weekend. When Grandma Berny was busy, Leah's brother Jacob, five years younger than Leah, had to tag along and chased his own little ball up and down the sidelines. Football was in the blood, it seemed.

'My coaches say I'm doing pretty well,' Leah reported back to her parents after training one day. 'I've just got to keep working hard.'

Hard work had never been a problem for Leah. She trained harder than any of the young footballers at the academy and listened carefully to every last instruction the coaches gave her. Combined with her natural talent, her efforts were beginning to pay off. In the two seasons since she'd joined Rushden and Diamonds, she had come on in leaps and bounds.

CHAPTER 3

HIGHBURY HAPPINESS

Leah decided early on that she was going to support Arsenal, like her mum and gran before her. Dad had taken her along to Spurs for her first game and even bought his five-year-old daughter a kit, but Tottenham just weren't the team for her.

'Sorry, Dad,' said Leah, handing him back the shirt. 'But Arsenal are waaaay better!'

After much pleading, Mum agreed to take Leah to her first Arsenal match at Highbury Stadium in North London. Watching on TV just wasn't the same and Leah was never allowed to stay up for *Match of the Day*.

When the tickets dropped through the letterbox

one morning, Leah's eyes were wide in excitement. 'Thank you! Thank you! Thank you!' she said.

'Only six more sleeps to go,' Mum said, smiling. She was almost as excited as Leah. And Grandma Berny was the most excited of all!

Then one sunny August afternoon, near the start of the new season, the day of the match arrived.

To get to the stadium, they had to take the train into London from Milton Keynes to Euston, then the Tube to Highbury and Islington station. As they boarded the train that Saturday, more Arsenal fans joined the carriage too, dressed in red-and-white-striped scarves and bobble hats with the club's crest sewn on.

Leah was wearing her favourite Arsenal home shirt with 'Henry 14' printed on the back – she only ever took it off at bedtime. Not one of the fans on board the train could have predicted that Arsenal would go the whole season unbeaten, earning them the nickname of the 'Invincibles', as well as the Premier League trophy. No team had got through the season without losing at least one match for decades!

They got off the Tube with an hour to go until kick-off. Plenty of time to look at the stalls that lined the streets on the way to the ground.

'We've got to get you a scarf to remember your first match,' said Berny. She slipped a five-pound note into a stallholder's hand in exchange for a long stripy scarf.

Leah draped it around her neck before Mum took a photo on her new phone. Happiness beamed out of Leah's little face like sunbeams.

'Programmes! Get your programmes!' a man shouted, holding up a copy of the matchday magazine in the air. Leah's favourite player, forward Thierry Henry, was the cover star, so Mum bought a copy to read on the journey home.

Through the turnstiles the family went, before they found their seats in the lower tier of the West Stand alongside lots of other young Arsenal fans and their parents. They had a great view of the pitch and had picked the end where the home team were warming up.

'Look, there he is!' said Gran, pointing to a tall player stood with hands on hips, ready to take a shot at goal.

Wow! It's really him, thought Leah. Thierry Henry is right there in front of us! She couldn't wait to tell her friends at training.

There were no goals in the first half, until just before the hour mark when Arsenal opened the scoring at last.

Goooooooaaaaaaallllllllll!!!!

The noise inside Highbury Stadium was like nothing Leah had ever heard. She jumped up and down before giving her mum and grandma two huge hugs.

The goalscorer was Sol Campbell, a defender who had moved from rivals Tottenham Hotspur a couple of seasons earlier. The Spurs fans still hadn't forgiven him!

'Dad is not going to be happy!' said Leah with a cheeky smile.

They had picked a good match for Leah's first game – Arsenal looked like they were going to win. Play continued with Arsenal creating more chances, but they couldn't add to their score.

'*One-nil to the Arsenal, One-nil to the Arsenal. . .*' The crowd sang the club's famous song.

Towards the end of the match, fans began shuffling past Leah and her family towards the exits.

'Where's everyone going?' Leah asked, puzzled. There were still five minutes left to play – anything could happen yet!

'Don't worry, we're staying right here,' Mum replied. Leaving early to beat the queues for the Tube wasn't an option for super fans Amanda and Berny. They would rather queue for an extra hour than miss even a minute's play.

Then right on the stroke of full-time, their loyalty was rewarded.

Dutchman Dennis Bergkamp won a fifty-fifty ball with a defender and chipped a pass forwards to Thierry Henry. The keeper rushed out but missed the ball completely! The angle was tight, but Thierry had the whole goal to aim at – he easily slotted home to the delight of the Highbury crowd. 2–0!

'Yesssssss!' cheered Leah, dancing on her red plastic seat.

Three points for Arsenal and her hero Henry had scored too! Leah had loved every moment of her first trip to Highbury. She skipped out of the stadium, holding hands with Mum and Gran on either side.

'That was amazing!' said Leah, the adrenaline still buzzing through her body. 'When can we go again?'

'That depends . . .' teased Grandma Berny. 'Are you definitely a Gooner?'

'I definitely am!' Leah promised. 'Ooh to, ooh to be, Ooh to be a GOO-NER!'

She knew all the chants already!

CHAPTER 4

A YOUNG GUNNER

After that first game, Leah was well and truly hooked. She had fallen in love with Arsenal Football Club and by now knew all the names of the men's players, from wonderkid Jérémie Aliadière to centre-forward Sylvain Wiltord.

Whenever she got any pocket money it was spent on football stickers, with any doubles handed down to Jacob. 'Got, got, need,' she would check through each packet. She liked the shinies best!

'When I grow up, I'm going to play for Arsenal,' Leah told her teacher at Portfields School one day.

Her teacher looked puzzled. 'I'm not sure girls are allowed to play in the Premier League,' he said, trying his best to let her down gently.

Leah knew that she would probably have to get a job too – Mum and Dad explained that there wasn't a professional league for women like the men's just yet – but that didn't mean she couldn't play for Arsenal.

What Leah's teacher didn't know was that the club had another team just as strong as the men's side. Arsenal Ladies were unstoppable! And they had a girls' Academy.

So, when Leah learned that her favourite Diamonds' coach was leaving to work at Arsenal's Centre of Excellence, her imagination went into overdrive. At first, she begged her not to go, until the coach made Leah an offer that was almost too good to be true.

'Once I'm settled, we'll get you along to Arsenal for a trial,' her coach promised. It wasn't like she was doing Leah a favour, as the nine-year-old was certainly talented enough to try out for Arsenal's Under-10s.

Leah couldn't believe her luck. 'Just imagine, Mama . . . Arsenal! The club where Thierry Henry plays! The club I've supported my whole life!'

'Let's keep everything crossed then,' said Mum.

In the meantime, schoolwork kept Leah busy. As always, homework was handed in on time and reading books were never left unfinished. Football remained just a hobby.

A couple of weeks later, Leah was invited for the trial she had been promised. What's more, it was being held at Highbury. By now Arsenal's men had moved to a shiny new stadium, less than a mile away from their previous home.

Leah felt like her nerves were about to bubble over as she arrived there with Mum. It felt unbelievable that she was being given the chance to play football on the very same pitch where she had watched her heroes. When she tried to imagine actually signing for the same club as Thierry Henry or the captain Patrick Vieira, it sent shivers down her spine!

As she stepped onto the enormous pitch, Leah realised she was the only girl not dressed in full Arsenal kit – the other girls already belonged to the Academy.

I can't worry about looking like the odd one out,

Leah told herself sensibly. She knew it was her one chance to impress.

The trial went by in a flash. Leah cut out every dangerous ball she could and stood firm in every tackle. At the end of the session, she shook hands with teammates and opposition players, and thanked the coaches. Impressive for a nine-year-old!

'Did you enjoy that?' her old coach asked after the session. 'The players are stronger here than at Diamonds, but you did really well.'

And she had. Once Leah had stepped foot on that pitch, she had aced her trial. 'Yeah, it was amazing,' she replied.

Then the coach smiled. 'Well, that's good, because we'd like you to join us at Arsenal next season if you'd like?'

'Like'? This is the best thing that's happened in my whole life! thought Leah. 'I would *love* to!' she cried.

'Thank you!' said Amanda, giving the coach a crushing handshake and her daughter an even bigger squeeze. 'We'll see you next season then!'

*

It had taken Dad a little while to get used to the idea, but in the end, he had no choice. He had to accept that his only daughter was Arsenal through and through. When she wasn't playing for the club, she was watching as a fan at the new Emirates Stadium.

He'd seen the way his daughter's eyes had lit up when she'd been given a bag full of brand-new kit at the Academy. Being a Gunner made her so happy, even if her new Number 6 shirt did nearly go down to her knees!

He'd cheer for his daughter when he came to see her in action, but he could never bring himself to say the name of his North London rivals.

He hoped they could take a break from football on their family holiday to Cornwall.

They were just in the middle of a game of beach cricket when Mum's phone rang. It was someone from the club, asking whether Leah would like to be a mascot for the men's team.

'There's just one problem,' said Mum. 'The match is away to West Brom.'

'That's halfway across the country!' said Dad.

Looking into Leah's pleading eyes, her parents realised that they didn't have much choice. This would make Leah's month, her whole year in fact!

So, the next morning Mum and Leah set off on the long drive to the Hawthorns. They joined the rest of the family back in Cornwall the day after the match. Leah had loved every minute of being a mascot and was bursting to tell Dad and Jacob all about it.

'I even had a photo with Theo!' she beamed.

Theo Walcott was the club's new teenage winger who had been to the World Cup with England aged just seventeen. He was a great role model for Leah, but he wasn't the only one.

Arsenal's women's first team was the best in the land. With Rachel Yankey on the wing, Kelly Smith up front and a young Alex Scott who could play anywhere on the right, they won trophy after trophy after trophy. The trio starred for England too!

When Leah was ten, she had another chance to be mascot, when England's women played in an important World Cup qualifier. A signed photo of Leah standing proudly next to her Arsenal and

England hero Kelly Smith became her most treasured possession.

To Leah,
Dream big!!!
Best wishes,
Kelly Smith 10

Leah read those words every day. She would love to play for Arsenal and England some day, but she knew that 'Dreaming big' would count for nothing if she didn't work hard. And just like Kelly, Leah was ready to do whatever it took to be the best footballer she could be.

CHAPTER 5

VERY IMPORTANT VISITORS

27 April 2007, Arsenal Training Centre

After school at the Academy one day, heavy April showers forced the girls to train indoors. Leah would have rather been out on the grass any day, but as long as she had a football at her feet, she was happy.

While the girls stopped for a quick drink break, Leah worked on her kick-ups. *Right-foot – ninety-seven, left-foot – ninety-eight, head – ninety-nine . . .*

'Woah!' gasped one of her Academy teammates, staring over towards the door. 'You might want to stop now.'

But Leah carried on. 'You can go next,' she said,

never taking her eyes off the ball for a second. 'Ten more and I'll beat my record!'

What Leah didn't realise was that the entire Arsenal women's team had just filed into the sports hall. Usually, they didn't arrive at training until later in the evening, after they had all finished their day jobs, but that day manager Vic Akers had called them in early for one last training session ahead of the biggest match in their history – the UEFA Women's Cup Final.

That season, Arsenal were chasing the quadruple. They had wowed crowds all season long, winning the League and the League Cup along the way. No English team had ever reached the UEFA Women's Cup Final before, let alone won four titles in the same season. If they won that and the FA Cup a couple of weeks later, this Arsenal squad would write their names into the history books forever!

The following afternoon they were set to play the second leg of the European final. The first leg, away to Swedish champions Umeå had been a nail-biting game. Alex Scott had left it late, scoring in injury time to secure a priceless 1–0 win. Advantage Arsenal.

Meanwhile in the sports hall, Leah was still going.

Right-knee – one hundred and nine, left-foot – one hundred and ten . . .

She was mid-kick when she suddenly felt a tap on her shoulder. 'Are we having a game or what?' a voice said with a giggle.

And standing there was the goalscorer herself – Alex Scott! Leah stopped suddenly and the ball bounced off across the hall.

'Um, if you like . . .' Leah stuttered.

Wingers Rachel Yankey, Karen Carney and more star players jogged over to join in.

'You can put us through our paces before our big match,' said Rachel Yankey. 'This is Alex, Kaz and you can call me Yanks,' she said, introducing the team.

The girls knew they had no chance against Arsenal's women – they were some of the best players on the planet – but they accepted the challenge anyway. It wasn't every day you got to share a pitch with your heroes!

Leah marvelled at just how good they were, zipping

passes to each other as fast as lightning. Their brains seemed to work at double speed and their feet worked even faster. Even so, the girls did manage to steal the ball a couple of times.

'You lot are pretty good!' said Karen, catching a chip from Leah with both hands. She turned to her teammates. 'What do we think, ladies? Shall we ask them?'

Ask us what? Leah wondered, not daring to say the words out loud.

Alex smiled. 'How would you all like to come down to Meadow Park and be our lucky mascots for the game?' she asked.

Wow! Leah tingled with excitement. By now, she had been a mascot a few times before, but never in a final, where her team might get to lift a trophy. The match was on a Sunday afternoon too – no school. Mum and Dad had to say yes!

And luckily for Leah, they did!

By the afternoon of the match the next day, the rain had moved on. Instead, it was a warm, clear day as Leah and her teammates lined up patiently to lead the players onto the pitch. The girls were all dressed in their red Arsenal home shirts, white shorts and white socks, and each had been given a mini football to show off their skills in front of a crowd of almost 3,500 fans. After a little kickaround, the girls would take their places in the stands to watch the action.

They were under strict instructions to cheer as loudly as possible. 'We'll need all the fans on our side to get us through the next ninety minutes,' captain Jayne Ludlow had told them earlier.

Even a goal up from the first leg, Arsenal were still the underdogs. Umeå had reached three European finals already, winning two of those, while it was Arsenal's very first final. The Swedish side had matchwinners all over the pitch too – not least Marta, a brilliant Brazilian, and teenage striker Ramona Bachmann, who were both deadly in front of goal.

Meanwhile Arsenal were without their own star goalscorer – Kelly Smith was suspended for both legs of the final. Disaster!

With the odds firmly stacked against them, Arsenal kicked off. As expected, Umeå attacked early on, but

Arsenal held their ground, seeing plenty of the ball themselves.

The Gunners' keeper Emma Byrne made a brilliant diving save towards half-time to keep her team ahead overall. Arsenal were still alive and kicking! They piled on the pressure in the second half, with Jayne Ludlow heading chances over the bar and another wide.

Umeå fought back though, and Emma again saved well from Ramona Bachmann, before she and Marta peppered the Arsenal goal again with more testing shots. Two minutes from time, Marta came closest yet to scoring, when she saw her twenty-yard free kick cannon back off the crossbar. Arsenal's lead was hanging by a thread!

'Come on, Arsenal!' the crowd urged.

When the referee's assistant raised the board to show there were five minutes of added time, the girls all groaned at once.

'You can do this!' Leah bellowed to the players on the pitch.

By now, their nerves were almost as shredded as the fans'. But at last, the final whistle blew.

Peeeeeeeeeepppp!

Arsenal were champions of Europe!

From the noise that erupted around the stadium, you could have been forgiven for thinking you were at the Gunners' new Emirates Stadium rather than the mini Meadow Park.

As Arsenal lifted the trophy, tears of happiness welled in Leah's eyes. What a team, what an achievement! She felt so lucky to be watching these amazing women, these role models right there before her eyes. The only heroes the players on the pitch had had growing up had all been men.

Now Leah had a new goal – she wanted to become a European champion too! There was a long way to go before that might happen, but if she kept working hard . . .

One day, just maybe! Leah began to dream.

CHAPTER 6

SCOUTED BY ENGLAND

During her early teenage years, Leah saw many young players come and go at Arsenal's Academy. She was always sad to see friends leave, but it helped her to stay humble. Things seemed to change in the blink of an eye and Leah didn't want the same thing to happen to her. A few of the reasons why players didn't make the cut were:

They were too small or slow.

They didn't work hard enough or show enough respect.

Some chose parties or friends over sport.

And sometimes, their changing bodies caused some girls to sadly give up altogether. Physical discomfort could make football tricky.

Leah knew this only too well, but her body always felt better after exercise. She was right where she wanted to be, loving every minute at the Academy. Playing as a central midfielder, she always looked comfortable on the ball. As she went up through the age groups, she worked tirelessly to improve her skills and technique each season.

The coaches were pleased with Leah's progress too. She was a player who led by example – always the first to check on a teammate if they got injured or rally to her side if they went a goal behind. A natural captain.

By now, she was on the radar of England's youth coaches, but the competition for places in the national side was famously fierce. Playing for England was a dream that only came true for the most talented players in the whole country. So, when five of Leah's Academy teammates had been selected to attend an England camp without her, it had hit hard.

'Keep going and you'll be next,' one of the Academy coaches said, trying to lift her spirits. He had no doubt that Leah was destined for great things.

So, Leah carried on training, working hard and learning all the time. She decided to concentrate on being the best she could be for her club and put her dreams of playing for her country to one side.

That way, if England did come calling, it would be a bonus.

Then, in 2012, a first call-up for the young Lionesses did arrive! Leah was chosen to train with England's Under-15s squad.

When Amanda read the email, she almost burst. 'My daughter, an England star!' she screamed.

The whole family wanted to celebrate Leah's achievement!

Leah meanwhile stayed quiet. It would be a big step up, facing some of the best players in the whole country. She would also have to stay away from home for three whole days and nights. And this time, she was the only girl from Arsenal going. She felt lonely already.

When the time came, Mum dropped her daughter off at England's training base, giving her a big hug for luck. 'You've got this, bubba!' she said proudly.

Leah knew how lucky she was to have a family who never stopped believing in her. This moment was as special for them as it was for her. At times, it was their pride that kept her going.

On the first morning of camp, Leah was up and ready to go. She headed to the pitches ten minutes early, keen to make a good impression. But she wasn't the only one. Striding ahead of Leah were three girls dressed in the sleek black England training kits they had all been given.

Leah slowed her pace a little and fixed her eyes on one girl with strawberry-blonde hair carrying a bag of footballs almost as big as she was over her shoulder. Laughing and joking, the girl looked so calm compared to Leah, who suddenly felt homesickness start to creep over her.

Once on the pitch, the girl took out a ball and began practising short, sharp passes to her friends, adding a flick or a trick each time she touched the ball.

Leah watched from the sidelines, wowed. *Her*

technique is amazing! If I'm going to get through this camp, I have to make that girl my friend! she resolved.

As the girl caught her eye, Leah pretended to need a long swig of water from her drinks bottle.

'You going to join us any time?' said the girl in a strong northern accent.

'Erm, sure,' said Leah, hoping her crimson cheeks would go unnoticed.

So Leah joined in, feeling like the geekiest teenager in the world. *If only they knew about my* Star Wars *bedcovers back home!* She pushed the thought out of her mind.

The girl introduced herself as Keira Walsh. She played for Blackburn Rovers' academy in the north of England. Just like Leah, Keira had loved going to matches since she was tiny too and her family were all mad Manchester City fans.

From day one, Leah and Keira hit it off. After that, the first thing both girls would do was look for each other's name on the squad list whenever an England camp was announced. Having a friend there made things so much easier when the team was far from home.

By the time they turned seventeen, within days of each other, Leah and Keira had become inseparable. On the pitch, meanwhile, they had blossomed into two of the most promising young players in the country. Keira was a brilliant midfielder who could read the game as well as anyone Leah had ever known, while Leah found her maturity and kindness earned her the role of the Young Lionesses' captain.

Wherever this football journey might take them, Leah and Keira were so glad to be on it together.

CHAPTER 7

ONE OF OUR OWN

Leah was still sixteen when Arsenal's pre-season training in 2014 began. Shelley Kerr, the head coach of the first team, had watched Leah's progress in the Academy closely and liked what she saw. In the space of just a few months, Leah had made great strides.

That season, Arsenal were hit by a double whammy – a few of their stars had just retired, while a string of injuries hit at precisely the wrong time. The team had a busy schedule ahead, with big matches to play in the league as well as two cup competitions and the Champions League. Shelley needed to boost her squad and decided to put her faith in some of the Academy's brightest stars. It was an Arsenal tradition to develop young players and the fans loved a homegrown hero!

So, when Leah was named as Arsenal's Number 14 for the season ahead – the same number that Thierry Henry had once worn – it was a dream come true! Her promotion to the first-team squad had come earlier than expected, but the midfielder was ready to shine.

Leah knew that training with her heroes every day would really help her game. These were top players she could really learn from. Kelly Smith, Rachel Yankey – she couldn't help but feel starstruck. It was Arsenal's right-back Alex Scott who took Leah under her wing, offering tips and advice to help the youngster settle into the side.

'You've got the skill to hold on to the ball,' Alex told Leah in training. 'Don't be in such a rush to give it away again.'

'Got it!' said Leah.

'Much better,' said Alex. 'Now look for Yanks on the wing.'

Leah made the pass as instructed. She was so grateful to Alex for taking the time to help her learn and improve.

On Leah's seventeenth birthday, 29 March 2014, Shelley gave her a present she would never forget. Leah and Mum were shopping in London, when the Arsenal coach phoned.

'I want you on the bench tomorrow,' Shelley told Leah. 'You've earned this chance.'

Leah couldn't believe what she was hearing! She might get to make her Arsenal debut the day after turning seventeen. And this wasn't just any match – it was the Champions League quarter-final! The birthday celebrations would have to be put on hold.

Birmingham City were already 1–0 up from the first leg and added two more goals in the first half at Meadow Park. There was no coming back from this, now Arsenal were playing for pride.

'Okay, Leah,' said Shelley sending on her sub. 'Stay relaxed on the ball – play *your* game.'

Leah nodded nervously. She had tied and untied her bootlaces at least three times.

I'm not sure I'm actually ready for this, she wanted to tell her coach. It was tempting to stay in the stands and watch, but Leah knew she had a job to do. *I'm a footballer now, not a fan*, she told herself.

'You've got this, kid!' said Yanks, high-fiving Leah onto the pitch as she made her exit.

In the ten minutes left, Leah couldn't help her side get a goal back, but they didn't let in any more goals. And once on the grass, her nerves had soon melted away.

Arsenal were out of the Champions League, but now they had to salvage their season and give the fans something to sing about. Sadly, they found themselves bottom of the Women's Super League, sending shockwaves around the league. Arsenal were used to winning – they had never been in the relegation zone before!

A good performance in the FA Cup final against Everton would be more important than ever. Was it fate that the match was played at Stadium MK in Milton Keynes, Leah's hometown? Only the year before, Leah had won the FA Youth Cup with Arsenal and laid out her dream to win the real thing someday. Now her dream that had seemed so distant could already be about to come true. It was like a fairy tale.

'This time, it's the big one!' Leah said to Mum ahead of the match.

'We're behind you all the way,' Mum encouraged.

By now Leah had more experience under her belt, from playing in the league. A player so young, she was bound to make mistakes, but she was learning from every game and her teammates treated her as an equal.

Arsenal were favourites for the game and started in style. Fifteen minutes in, Kelly Smith curled a cracking free kick beyond the desperate dive of the keeper.

'Go on, Kelly!' Leah cheered from the bench.

Next, after sixty minutes, the striker set up Yukari Kinga to score her first Arsenal goal. What a player!

By the time Leah joined the party from the bench, the whole team was buzzing. Arsenal weren't the record holders of the FA Cup for nothing and now they had another trophy to add to their collection. Everton were defeated. Final score 2–0.

Leah had won her first silverware with Arsenal in

her very first season! What a day! *This is a moment I'll never forget*, she said to herself.

Soon it was trophy time. Captain Kelly raised the silver cup dressed in red ribbons to the delight of the cheering crowd. And when the team posed for their winners' photo, Leah's smile was the biggest beam of all. She had experienced a remarkable rise from fan to mascot to FA Cup winner in her short career so far.

Sadly, the match was Shelley Kerr's last in charge. Her team had been desperate to send their coach out in style.

The victory spurred Arsenal on to turn their season around; they climbed the league table and made the League Cup final too.

Disappointingly, a second trophy wasn't to be that season, as Manchester City sneaked a 1–0 win in Wycombe. Arsenal were unlucky to lose and this time Leah played the full final.

It ended a brilliant breakthrough year for Leah. The midfielder had been worried when Shelley Kerr had left, but her new manager Pedro Martínez Losa saw the same special qualities in Leah that Shelley had done.

'This girl has a bright future ahead of her,' Pedro announced to the press.

And by the end of the season, Leah had become a fan favourite too:

'She's one of our own,
She's one of our own,
Leah Williamson,
She's one of our own.'

That song would never get old!

CHAPTER 8

NERVES OF STEEL

Since Leah's first England call-up, she had been chosen for every camp. She was growing as a player and impressing the coaches with her stylish play. In her debut season with Arsenal, she had been voted England Women's Youth Player of the Year, and by the time she was eighteen she had made the England youth captaincy her own.

In the spring of 2015, Leah's team of Young Lionesses travelled to Belfast, Northern Ireland, to take part in a mini tournament. If they did well, they would qualify for the Women's Under-19 Championship that summer in Israel.

'I've never been to Israel before,' her teammate

Katie Zelem pondered, during the team's short flight to Belfast.

'Neither have I, but we can't think about that yet,' Leah replied.

Although she was confident about the games in Belfast, Leah was a player who didn't like to look too far into the future. If England didn't perform against Norway, Northern Ireland and Switzerland, they wouldn't be going anywhere that summer.

The first match against Norway was the toughest of the ties. England found themselves 1–0 down after an hour. The girls pushed for the equaliser, but with just minutes left on the clock scored an unfortunate own goal. Disaster! There was just time for Rosella Ayane to pull one back for England but they still trailed until – *peeeep!* – they were awarded a penalty kick deep into added time!

Leah was on penalty duties that day. There was no one the team trusted more than their calm captain. She picked up the ball and placed it on the spot. She could see the keeper clapping her hands together and jumping to touch the crossbar, trying to make herself look big in an effort to put Leah off. It didn't work though – Leah made up her mind exactly where to place the ball and smashed it past the keeper.

'Yesssss, Leah!' cheered her teammates, running over to celebrate.

But the ref wasn't happy – Rosella had entered the area before the penalty had been struck. She blew her whistle loudly. No goal! Then to everyone's amazement, a free kick to Norway was awarded.

Leah tried to protest without losing her cool. 'Ref! Surely I get to take it again?' she explained.

But the referee wouldn't listen, even though she had made the wrong decision! Seconds later, she blew again for full time. England had lost 2–1.

'I don't understand,' said Leah, walking off the pitch. 'I should have been given a second chance.' She was only eighteen, but she knew the rules of football inside out.

'Don't worry,' said the England coach Mo Marley. 'We'll be putting in an official complaint.'

The next day, there came a very strange decision. England were ordered to take the penalty against

Norway again and play the rest of the game – all twelve seconds of it! It wouldn't be played until five days later, on the same day as England's final match against Switzerland. A new referee would take charge, with the original ref sent home from the tournament for her error.

Leah was in for a long wait before she could take her penalty again. Five whole days! The teenager felt sick.

Mum changed her flight home so she could be there for the Norway match.

'I'm not going anywhere,' she promised.

Next, England had Northern Ireland to play. This match finished England 9, Northern Ireland 1. Much easier! Leah converted two more perfect penalties, with her teammates making sure to stay out of the way.

In between matches, Leah tried to sleep as much as possible, but found herself pacing up and down the corridors of the hotel. All she could think about was retaking that Norway penalty.

The captain scored yet again from the spot in their

next match against Switzerland, as England ran out winners. But Norway won their game too and led the group. If Leah missed her penalty against them, England wouldn't qualify for the final tournament. Now the pressure felt too much to bear.

That evening, the same teams for England and Norway prepared to finish what they had started.

In the dressing room, the mood was quiet. There wasn't the usual pre-match buzz of excitement. Leah sat on the bench looking pale.

'I could take it,' Katie offered kindly. She could see that Leah was suffering and there wasn't any rule that said another player couldn't take the penalty.

'Thanks,' said Leah. 'But this is something I have to do myself.' She was the captain – she had to take one for the team.

Even though the match would last for less than a minute, the teams still had to go through a full warm-up. The last thing they wanted was for someone to get injured.

Leah placed the ball on the spot and walked back to the edge of the box. Hands on hips, she stared down the keeper. The stand behind the goal was completely empty. Then up stepped Leah and *gooooooaaaaallllll!* The keeper dived the other way.

Her teammates all piled on. 2–2!

'Wow, that was worse than taking my driving test!' said Leah, the smile returning to her face at last.

'You've got nerves of steel!' Katie said, hugging her captain, whose legs had suddenly turned to jelly.

But wait, England still had twelve seconds left to play! Thankfully, that wasn't enough time for Norway to score. The Young Lionesses held on to leapfrog Norway at the top of the group – they were going to Israel after all! What an achievement!

Leah picked up the match ball. 'Can I keep this, please?' she asked.

The ref nodded. It was the only match ball Leah had ever wanted, a memento that would remind her of passing such a tricky test.

It was after midnight by the time the girls were back in their hotel rooms. Leah should have been exhausted, but the adrenalin just wouldn't leave her body. While her teammates slept soundly, Leah lay on the bathroom floor. Still dressed in her full kit, she rested her head on the football and scrolled through video after video on YouTube. Her phone was filled with messages of support from family and friends, but she wasn't ready to read them just yet.

I can't wait to retire so I don't have to go through this again, the unwanted thought wouldn't leave her head. Leah loved football more than anything, but she wouldn't have wished that five-day wait on her worst enemy. Some days the pressures that came with the sport were unbearable.

After that, Leah sought some help. The young footballer had learned an important lesson – she didn't have to try to cope with everything on her own. Her family, coaches and teammates were all there to help; all Leah had to do was ask.

CHAPTER 9

BATTLING BACK

Leah's debut season with Arsenal had been magical. She had gone from teenage zero to Arsenal hero in the space of a few short months! Her coaches loved her and so did her teammates. And before she knew it, she had completed her first season as a proper footballer.

At their family home in Newport Pagnell, Leah and Mum were looking through a scrapbook Mum had made. It contained all Leah's match reports and some priceless photos too. It was nice to look back on how far Leah had come in her first year as a senior footballer.

'Here's when you'd just scored your first Arsenal

goal!' Mum said, smiling.

That had come when Arsenal thrashed Millwall in the League Cup. Kelly Smith had had a spooky feeling that Leah would score that day, even though the teenager was playing left-back.

When Leah received the ball from Yanks just before half-time in the match, nothing was stopping her. She turned and shook off two defenders before launching a rocket from outside the box. *Gooooooaaaaaaallll!*

'When Kelly told me I was going to score, then I had to score!' Leah joked.

'That goal was sick!' said her little brother Jacob, sliding onto the sofa next to them. He had watched the clip so many times on YouTube, he knew the commentary off by heart!

'What a way to announce yourself on the senior stage,' Jacob mimicked. 'Take a bow, Leah Williamson!' He still didn't understand why she hadn't pulled out a crazy goal celebration though – Leah had looked ice-cold!

Now as the new season was about to kick off, Leah received the best eighteenth birthday present she could wish for – her first professional contract with Arsenal. Sometimes she had to pinch herself, to check that it wasn't all just a dream. But no – this was Leah's life now, all her efforts on the pitch had rightly earned her a contract.

Her fine performances for England's youth teams had not gone unnoticed either, with the coaches keeping a close eye on the Arsenal ace. The year 2015 was a World Cup year with the Lionesses set to head to Canada for the tournament. And although she hadn't played for England's senior team before, Leah's name had been added to a longlist of players in contention for the squad.

Wow! She couldn't imagine what it would feel like to play at a World Cup. What an amazing adventure that would be. She may have only been eighteen, but Leah remembered that Australia's Caitlin Foord was only sixteen when she made her World Cup debut in the last tournament. Maybe it wasn't such an impossible dream?

In the end, the England boss Mark Sampson contacted Leah before the squad was announced. He had decided that the World Cup would come too soon for the teenager this time, but her opportunity to shine would not be far away.

'Keep working hard and we'll talk again,' he told her.

'I will,' Leah promised.

In the end, five of her Arsenal teammates made the squad: Siobhan Chamberlain, Alex Scott, Casey Stoney, Jordan Nobbs and Lianne Sanderson, all top players who could make a difference in big matches. Leah didn't feel too disappointed, though. Instead, she was excited to watch England's matches as a fan.

Soon after though, Leah suffered the first serious setback of her career, when she snapped the ligaments in her ankle. The injury would keep her out for months. Leah was devastated – football had become her whole life and now it had been cruelly taken away.

'It's a good job I'm not going to Canada,' she told the Arsenal physio. 'I would have felt a hundred times worse.'

'Don't worry, we'll get you back on your feet,' the physio told her.

It was the first bump in the road on Leah's football journey. Now months of work on the physio table and in the gym lay ahead. Off the pitch, Leah had her A-level exams to take too: history, PE and her favourite subject – maths. It was a tough time, but Leah got through it.

England returned from the World Cup as heroes with shiny bronze medals – their best-ever finish at the tournament. Sampson's squad had come agonisingly close to reaching the final itself, only for their dream to be shattered by an own goal in stoppage time against Japan. Still, the Lionesses had made their country proud.

And before long, Leah was back from injury too, feeling refreshed and ready to tackle the end of the season.

CHAPTER 10

WEMBLEY AWAITS

Back when she had made her debut, Leah had been surprised by the pace of the Women's Super League – the speed of the game was so quick. The moment she got the ball, one or two players would put her under pressure straightaway. As a young player, she knew she wasn't the finished product, but she was a fast learner. She wouldn't make the same mistake twice if she could help it and she felt terrible if ever she let her team down.

At the age of nineteen, Leah had gone from wonderkid to wonder woman. She was faster and stronger than she ever had been before and could match the top players stride for stride.

For Arsenal's pre-season tour to Spain that year, coach Pedro had a new position in mind for Leah. He wanted to try her out as a centre-back, in the heart of the Gunners' defence. Leah wasn't happy.

'Why won't he play me in midfield?' she sulked, as the team were warming up.

Yanks smiled. 'You're strong in midfield, but you'd make an even better defender. . .' she said honestly. 'A natural.'

Leah began to wonder. *Maybe I should try defence?* This was Arsenal after all, her club. If truth be told, she would probably have gone in goal if it meant she got to play!

Being a defender turned out to be much less boring than Leah had imagined. She read the game so well that she rarely had to make any last-ditch tackles. Pedro let her start more games and she had a fantastic teacher to show her the ropes: Casey Stoney was an England centurion!

Arsenal made a good start in the league, but one of their goals was to reach another FA Cup final – that year the trophy would be decided at Wembley Stadium for only the second time in the women's game. None of the players had ever imagined they would get the chance to play at the famous stadium, even the younger players like Leah and Katie McCabe.

'Opportunities like this don't come around too often,' said Kelly at the start of their FA Cup run. 'Let's get to Wembley and return that trophy to its rightful owners!'

'Yesssss!' the girls all roared.

The season before, Chelsea had knocked Arsenal out of the cup in the quarter-finals and gone on to beat Manchester City in the final. Now it was time to take back the trophy.

Leah knew it might be the final trophy of Kelly's glittering career and desperately wanted the team to win it for her. Growing up, Kelly was the definition of a hero to Leah. She was so glad to have had the chance to play in the same team together. It would be an amazing fifth FA Cup for Kelly and an incredible fourteenth title for Arsenal if they won.

Just as they had planned, the Gunners did make the final, but they definitely achieved it the hard way.

They almost came unstuck against Birmingham in the fifth round, edging it on penalties, and spot-kicks again decided their quarter-final win over Notts County. After that, they sailed through their semi-final against Sunderland, winning 7–0, even though they were down to ten players for most of the match.

Now they faced the defending champions Chelsea in front of a crowd of 33,000 noisy fans. Leah couldn't wait!

When the big day arrived, the whole Williamson family were in the stands at Wembley Stadium. They wouldn't have missed it for the world.

I just hope I get some minutes, Leah worried. She knew how proud it would make her parents. What she was forgetting though was that they were already proud of her and how far she had come. She had achieved so much – it was easy to forget she was still just a teenager.

On the morning of the match, Mum phoned Leah with some final words for luck.

'We'll visit the stone on our way in,' Mum promised.

'Give it a rub for me!' Leah replied.

When Wembley Stadium had been rebuilt from scratch a few years earlier, Mum and Dad had bought a special Christmas present for their kids one year, a little piece of football history. Theirs was one of a few hundred stones laid on Wembley Way, engraved with special messages and dedications for fans. Mum and Dad's chosen words were simple but perfect:

LEAH AND JACOB,
BORN TO PLAY FOOTBALL

In the dressing room, goalkeeper Emma Byrne had a good feeling about the match. 'We're going to win today!' she said confidently.

'Right then, I'll enjoy it!' Leah laughed. Although she was on the bench, her main emotion was not disappointment, just being a part of that squad made her feel so happy. In fact, she was probably the happiest sub in the history of Arsenal Football Club!

Kelly laid down a marker in the first ten seconds of the match, producing a perfect slide tackle to win the ball for her side. Then soon after, Dan Carter delivered a sensational strike to give Arsenal the lead.

'Wow!' Leah gasped, as Dan's shot curled in at the far post.

Try as they might, Chelsea just couldn't break Arsenal down. In the dying minutes of the game, Leah came on to help shore up the defence. Now all they had to do was hold on.

But as the ball bounced towards Leah, she suddenly slipped. Luckily, it hit a Chelsea player next and went out for an Arsenal throw.

'Hey, Bambi,' said Casey, helping her up. 'Check you're wearing the right studs next time.'

How embarrassing! Leah's cheeks blazed red. *I guess I've still got a lot to learn.*

Then it was over. Arsenal had done it!

'*Campeones, campeones. . .*' the Arsenal fans burst into song.

And the players joined in: '*Olé, olé, olé!*'

Leah, meanwhile, couldn't hold back the tears. She had only been on the pitch for a few minutes, but she felt like she had kicked every ball from the bench.

Now she felt exhausted and emotional.

She headed straight to Mum in the crowd and climbed the barrier for a huge hug.

'Great game,' Mum congratulated Leah. 'Now go celebrate!'

CHAPTER 11

NORDIC CHAMPIONS

It wasn't long after that famous win at Wembley when Leah picked up another injury. It happened during the mid-season break, while Arsenal were out in Seattle in the United States. It was the first friendly match between a WSL side and a team from America's top flight, the NWSL. Seattle Reign (now known as OL Reign) would be the Gunners' opponents.

Just eight minutes into the clash, Leah had stayed down after a tackle. This time, it was her other ankle, and it didn't look good.

Her teammate Jordan Nobbs rushed over. 'Can you walk on it?' she asked.

'I don't think so,' cried Leah. 'Stupid glass ankles!'

So Leah left the pitch on a stretcher and was replaced by Alex. Was her season over, just as she was playing so well?

Almost as bad was being pushed through the airport in a wheelchair for the flight home. 'Your steering's terrible!' Leah joked to Jordan.

Surgery on Leah's ankle followed and while the operation went well, she was racked with worry. She had seen it happen before; some players never came back from an injury like this and now it had happened to her not once, but twice.

What if my ankle doesn't heal properly . . . will I lose my place in the team for good? she worried. *Pedro might easily forget about me.*

More months on the sidelines gave Leah the chance to think about things. She loved football, but what if injury struck again? Away from the game, she decided to study accountancy, so she could get a good job in case her football career went horribly wrong. She had always had a head for numbers at school.

As well as the books, Leah hit the gym until the day finally came when her ankle was strong enough to kick a football again. She came back stronger and wiser, and in 2017 started the season afresh with a new number too. When she heard she was changing back to her old Number 6 shirt, it felt like it was meant to be. Back in her Academy days, she had worn the number for a whole decade, even though she had hated it at first. Secretly she had wanted to be a flashy Number 10, until Mum bought her a pair of new Nike boots stitched with 'LW6' in red. And while the boots only lasted a season, 6 was a number she could grow into over the years.

*

By now Leah was twenty and was playing for England's Under-23s, the final squad before the senior side. A strong group of girls had grown up through the age groups together, but only the most talented of them would go on to become Lionesses. Leah was confident about her own chances, but would have to keep performing at her very best to earn a call-up.

That summer, the Young Lionesses were one of four teams set to contest the Nordic Cup in Sweden. Keen to make up for a trophy-less season with Arsenal,

Leah was excited to get away with England and catch up with some of her old friends. As always, Keira would make the camp a laugh and Leah's new Arsenal teammate Beth Mead was in the squad too. Ten days of football fun with friends and the chance to win a trophy at the end was Leah's idea of the perfect summer holiday.

England took on hosts Sweden first, winning comfortably 4–0.

Match two was against the United States, a nation that had produced some legends of the women's game. Their top league, the NWSL, was the best in the world. The game ended goalless, but England had happily kept a second clean sheet.

'One more good win and that trophy is ours, girls!' Leah said excitedly. She had played every minute so far in her favourite midfield role.

Their final opponents, Norway, were up next. At the back, England proved they had the meanest defence in the competition, while Hannah Blundell and Beth Mead scored a goal apiece to earn a 2–0 victory. They had done it – England were Nordic Cup champions!

'Ten days well spent to finish off the season. 6 goals + 3 clean sheets = Nordic Champions!' Leah wrote on her social media.

The girls were buzzing as they collected the cup! They deserved all the credit for their brilliant team performances against three top nations. This was a new generation of talent pushing for their first senior England call-ups, and time would tell as to who could go all the way.

CHAPTER 12

A LIONESS'S LEAP

Just a few months after their triumph in Norway, Leah and Keira were both named in England's senior squad for their World Cup qualifier, at home to Kazakhstan.

'Keira and Leah are both talented young players with lots of potential and are playing well for their clubs,' England's caretaker coach Mo Marley told the press.

'Yessssss!' Leah and Keira shared a huge hug when they heard of their selection.

Mo read out the team sheet at breakfast that day. Keira was named in midfield to win her first cap, while Leah was among the substitutes. It would have been natural for Leah to feel envious, but her emotions were the exact opposite. Instead, Leah would be Keira's number one fan, thrilled that her best friend would start. From the age of fourteen, they had shared everything on their footballing journey together: starting out as Young Lionesses, spells on the sidelines with similar ankle injuries, and now together at their first senior camp.

'This was written in the stars!' said Leah.

'Don't be soft!' Keira replied with affection. Leah was always the soppy one!

While Leah didn't get on that game, Keira played the full ninety minutes in a Fran Kirby-dominated 5–0 win.

'How did it feel?' Leah asked Keira, after the match.

'You're going to love it!' Keira replied, grinning.

By the spring of 2018, England had a new manager. Now all the players were starting from scratch – everyone would be bringing their A-game to impress Phil Neville. A former player with Manchester United and Everton, Phil had won multiple titles as well as the Champions League. He was joining England as a rookie coach, though, and had everything to learn about women's football.

Leah had previously worked under three Arsenal managers, each with their own coaching style and ideas about the game, but she had won over all three with her talent and winning attitude. Impressing a new England coach too? Challenge accepted!

For his first tournament, the SheBelieves Cup in the United States, Phil named a youthful squad. Leah was sadly ruled out of playing by a knee injury, but Phil decided to take her along anyway to settle her into the team. The Arsenal youngster would definitely feature in his future plans! The hosts won the tournament, with England finishing as runners-up.

Leah felt so lucky to have been a part of the squad, named alongside so many legendary Lionesses. Just like in her first season with Arsenal, she felt a little starry-eyed around the players.

By June that year, Leah was back to full fitness and ready to become a Lioness. Now a first-team regular at Arsenal, she was proving her quality week-in, week-out. Phil was impressed enough to ask Leah to join the squad for England's World Cup qualifier in Russia.

A plastic pitch wasn't the ideal surface, but England soon found themselves 2–0 up thanks to goals from Nikita Parris and Jill Scott. Russia struck back next to threaten England's lead, but Jill headed home her second goal before half-time. The second half saw Russia drop deeper, barely venturing out of their own half. Surely England were safe now.

With six minutes to go, Phil decided to give Leah her first taste of international football.

Remember to breathe, thought Leah, as the nerves bubbled up inside her.

'It's a straight swap with Keira once you've warmed up,' Phil explained.

Argh! thought Leah. *Anyone but Keira!* There was no way her best friend would be happy to be subbed. So, as Leah stood on the sidelines ready to take to the field, she practised her sternest game-face.

But she needn't have worried. When Keira spotted the electronic board showing that Leah's Number 14 would be coming on, she dashed straight over, with an enormous grin spread across her face.

'It had to be you!' joked Keira, as the pair

exchanged a quick hug.

'Who else?' laughed Leah, suddenly feeling emotional.

She hadn't had long to put her stamp on the game, but Leah had loved wearing the Lionesses shirt. Thankfully, more minutes weren't far away.

That October, England were away to Kazakhstan, in another World Cup qualifier. With their place in France sealed a few days earlier, the match gave Phil a chance to audition some of his Young Lionesses, including Leah, who would play from the start. And even better – she would wear the Number 6 shirt!

Usually, Mum and Dad would follow Leah anywhere to watch her play, but the flights to Russia and Kazakhstan were eye-wateringly expensive and would mean too much time off work.

'I suppose you've earned a free pass,' Leah told them. 'Just this once!'

'Take this with you,' said Mum. She pressed an envelope into Leah's hand and instructed her daughter to open it on the day of the match.

So, Leah did. Inside the envelope was a playing

card with the letter L in the middle and number 6s at the corners. It was the loveliest gift that Leah had ever received! A heartfelt message came with it. Even though the family would be thousands of miles apart, they would all be thinking of each other.

Back at home, Mum, Dad and Jacob had to watch the matches on a flickering internet stream. Women's football still had to catch up with the men's game in so many ways.

The Lionesses didn't let Phil down in Kazakhstan, roaring to a 0–6 scoreline, with five different goalscorers getting in on the action. Leah never looked troubled in the centre of England's defence and was pleased to help keep a clean sheet.

'Wow!' said Leah, walking off the pitch with Lucy Bronze at full time. 'That felt amazing.'

'That's good,' Lucy replied. 'Because it looks like plenty more caps will be heading your way.'

Leah certainly hoped so! Next year was a World Cup year and the Lionesses had already booked their spot. Was she good enough to join the likes of Lucy, Jill Scott and Ellen White in France? The Arsenal youngster would stay positive, keep working hard and see where that took her.

CHAPTER 13

TOP OF THE LEAGUE

When Australian coach Joe Montemurro took charge at Meadow Park in December 2017, Arsenal had high expectations. It was Joe's job to rebuild a squad that would make the Gunners great again, but it wouldn't be easy. By now some of their biggest stars – Casey Stoney, Kelly Smith, Rachel Yankey – had moved on to other clubs or hung up their boots for good, and Alex Scott would soon join that list too. Without any of those players' skills to call upon, it was up to a new generation at Arsenal to set the Women's Super League alight.

Along with their new Dutch striker Vivianne Miedema, Beth and Leah were among the club's brightest young players. But were they really ready to push for the title?

Growing up, Leah had watched Arsenal's unstoppable women crowned as champions almost every year, but they hadn't won the league since Leah was fifteen. Now it was London neighbours Chelsea who ruled the roost, under manager Emma Hayes.

When the new season got underway in 2018, Joe's first full season in charge, Arsenal made their intentions clear from day one. This season they would be brutal at the back and fearless up front. They would get the club back where it belonged.

Their opening match was a 5–0 victory over Liverpool at a noisy Meadow Park. Viv was a player with magic in her boots, a player who could hit a heroic hat-trick and add two assists in a single match. And that's just what she did against the Reds.

In October, Arsenal made the trip to Kingsmeadow to face defending champions Chelsea. Leah was steeled for a tight game. Kim Little netted a penalty before Viv and Jordan each scored twice. Arsenal had run riot, ending the Blues' two-year unbeaten home run. It was a stunning win, but the day was soured when a tackle from Drew Spence brought down Kim. Sadly, Arsenal's captain had broken her leg and would be out for months.

In the dressing room after the match, something changed. Arsenal's mentality went from 'we can win this league' to 'we *will* win this league'.

'We have to do it for Kim,' Leah stressed.

The next month though, Arsenal lost Jordan for the rest of the season through an Anterior Cruciate Ligament injury. Arsenal had won all their matches so far, but by December the squad was down to its bare bones – only nine outfield players were fully fit!

When they travelled to unbeaten Manchester City that month, Arsenal's luck ran out. Two Georgia Stanway goals sank the Gunners, cutting their lead at the top of the table to three points. But there were plenty of twists and turns in the title race still to come!

In January, Leah claimed her first league goal of the season in a win at West Ham United. When Beth delivered a perfect pass to the far post, it was Leah who leapt highest, planting a fine header past the keeper. *Gooooooaaaaalllll!*

But Arsenal lost again in the next match, when Chelsea, hungry for revenge, won at Meadow Park. It was a landmark game for Leah, but Chelsea's win had put a dampener on the celebrations.

'How does it feel to reach one hundred Arsenal appearances at the age of just twenty-one?' the press asked Leah.

'It's amazing to be up there in the company of my heroes, but I'm aiming to get a few hundred more yet with this football club,' she replied. On one hand, Leah was super proud to reach the milestone, but she couldn't help feeling she would have reached it even sooner were it not for two bad injuries.

And to lose that day felt painful. Now Manchester City were top of the league, although they had played one game more than Arsenal. Leah would use the disappointment at losing to drive her on.

'We've got to do better,' she resolved.

Arsenal's title hopes were temporarily boosted when Kim returned to the pitch, only for new signing

Lia Wälti to take Kim's place on the treatment table – again with a dreaded ACL injury.

Despite their threadbare squad, Arsenal got back to winning ways in their very next match. Viv set a new record for WSL goals at the end of January – sixteen – but the striker wasn't about to stop there.

England manager Phil Neville was in the crowd for Arsenal's away fixture at Liverpool, as the Gunners cruised to a 1–5 victory. Leah and Beth had done their chances of getting in the World Cup squad no harm at all!

'Leah Williamson will captain her country one day,' Phil told the press confidently, after the match. It was a bold claim to make – Leah was still only twenty-one – yet she had been sensational all season long at the heart of the meanest defence in the league.

In the next match, against Birmingham City, Arsenal had the chance to secure Champions League football for the first time in years. So when their Irish midfielder Katie McCabe scored the game's only goal – a cracking left-footed shot from the edge of the area – Leah couldn't hold back the tears. The Champions

League! It meant everything.

Then came Arsenal's chance to win the Women's Super League. The match was poised for a great occasion when Brighton moved the tie to the club's Falmer Stadium. Over 5,000 fans bought tickets – a new record for the WSL. Among the crowd were every relation that Leah had ever met, all there to hopefully witness the young Gunner's special moment.

When Viv scored with a spectacular strike in the sixth minute, Leah was almost crying again. Katie, Beth and Daniëlle van de Donk each chipped in with a goal after that, as Arsenal breezed to victory. 0–4.

Leah would be the first to admit that it was her worst performance in an Arsenal shirt – she just couldn't hold her emotions together. But that didn't matter now, City couldn't catch them – Arsenal were champions!

Now the happy tears flowed and flowed. Leah was a league champion with her childhood club, Arsenal. It didn't get better than that. Even Tottenham fan Dad was sobbing!

With the league done and dusted, Arsenal hosted Manchester City feeling invincible. It was a lovely touch when City gave the new champions a guard of honour before the match – it set the tone for what would be a perfect day. Arsenal left it late, but defender Emma Mitchell chose two minutes from time to hit the winner, with the best goal she would ever score!

'One-nil to the Arsenal!' the fans sung on repeat.

And when captain Kim lifted the trophy, the whole place erupted in delight.

What a season! Arsenal had delivered the goods for the fans at last.

CHAPTER 14

2019 WORLD CUP

Leah Williamson – league champion with Arsenal. It was going to take a while to sink in! It was the best season of her career so far. And not just for her club – a couple of months earlier, Leah had been chosen for England's SheBelieves Cup squad. The tournament was hosted by the world's number one side, the United States, and featured Brazil and Japan too, both brilliant on their day.

The atmosphere in the stadiums had made the hairs on Leah's arms stand on end. It was just how she imagined the atmosphere at a World Cup to be. She didn't get any minutes in the first two matches against Brazil and the United States, but she did make Phil's starting line-up for the Japan game. Having beaten Brazil and drawn against the United States, England could clinch the cup if they beat the 2011 world champions Japan. And they did! The Lionesses scored three times, while Leah helped to keep a clean sheet.

Incredible! England flew home on a high. They had won the trophy for the first time, and were unbeaten in all three matches against massive teams. To go to the States and win had felt amazing, and Leah was glad to have played her part, but it would count for nothing if they didn't perform on the biggest stage – at the 2019 Women's World Cup.

*

Leah was at a London shopping centre the day the World Cup squad was announced. After football, shopping was her favourite thing to do. Her fashion sense had come a long way since the days of only wearing football kits; now she styled designer bits with her best high-street buys.

BZZZZZ! Leah felt in her pocket for her phone. Keira's name flashed up on the screen.

'Have you read your email??!!' Keira shrieked down

the line.

Leah put Keira on speaker, as her phone began to buzz and ping uncontrollably.

'WE'RE GOING TO THE WORLD CUP!' Keira screamed.

The emotions hit Leah all at once. Shock, joy, but most of all pride. She'd longed with every cell in her body to be in that squad, but to actually hear the words . . .

'I can't believe it!' Leah gasped as the tears came fast.

'There's a video too,' Keira told her friend. 'Check it out!'

Normally the Football Association just sent out a squad list, but this time the team was made public on social media. An English celebrity had recorded a special video to announce each player.

First, Prince William confirmed the place of 'defensive rock' Steph Houghton, England's skipper for the tournament.

Wow! thought Leah. *A royal intro!* She watched on smiling, as more teammates were revealed. Kelly

Smith congratulated Beth on her place, while another Arsenal legend Ian Wright appeared next.

'Somebody that I've got a lot of admiration for, a fantastic player. . .' Wrighty began. 'Lifelong Arsenal supporter, Leah Williamson!'

Leah couldn't help it, she was gone! Shoppers tutted and gave disapproving glances as they passed, but Leah didn't even notice them.

*

5 June 2019, Nice, France

A choir of schoolchildren greeted the squad as they checked into their team hotel on Nice's Promenade des Anglais. Their rendition of 'Three Lions' was the perfect welcome to France! Not all that long ago Leah was their age, standing in awe before famous football players. The sunny Côte d'Azur would be England's base for the next few weeks, and the ideal place to relax whenever the girls had some downtime.

The tournament kicked off in style, with the pressure on favourites the United States and hosts France. The group games quickly came and went, with Leah an unused sub. England took maximum points against Scotland, Argentina and Japan, which made warming the bench easier for Leah to swallow. And it was such a strong, talented team!

'When the call comes, I need to be ready,' she said patiently.

In the last sixteen, England were drawn against Cameroon. Though 3–0 up before an hour had been played, the scoreline only told half the story. When the ref awarded a free kick for a back-pass to the Cameroon keeper, England's opponents were outraged. Steph stayed cool though, drilling the ball through a crowded goalmouth to open the scoring.

Next Lucy flicked the ball through to an unmarked Ellen White in the box, who easily slotted home. The ref blew for offside, but VAR decided that the goal should stand! England had scored fair and square, but Cameroon didn't agree. And when the team in green scored next, this time the goal was judged offside. The match was fast descending into chaos!

Alex Greenwood added a third for the Lionesses, before Cameroon escaped a penalty and a red card. Cool heads for the final minutes would be needed.

When Phil gestured for to Leah to come on, she put on her best game-face. Everything she had worked for had led her to this moment.

It meant the world to Leah, to know her whole family were in the crowd that applauded her onto the pitch. She thought of all the young girls and boys watching back home on TV too. It was magical.

Six minutes of normal time plus seven more of added time, and Leah's World Cup debut was over. The game had been scrappy and ugly, not exactly how she imagined her first tournament appearance would play out. Still, the fiery encounter was one she was unlikely to forget. And more importantly, England were through to the quarter-finals!

Leah didn't play against Norway, nor did she feature in the semi-final against the United States; Phil opted for experience over youth. England had come within a toe's length of equalising through Ellen, while Steph's scuffed penalty failed to take the game to extra time. Reigning champions the United States were into their third final in a row, while England were out. Heartbreaking.

While England's World Cup bid fell just short of winning a medal, this was a special squad. Talented, hardworking Lionesses! The players would carry the heartache into their next tournament, determined not to be on the losing side again.

CHAPTER 15

LESSON LEARNED

9 November 2019
Wembley Stadium, London

While Leah had won the FA Cup with Arsenal at Wembley, she had never played at the famous stadium in an England shirt. So, when a friendly fixture was announced after the World Cup, Leah kept everything crossed that she would feature in Phil's plans that day. To return there with England would be something special.

In fact, the Lionesses had only once played at Wembley before, back in 2014, when Germany were once again the opponents. Sadly, the European champions were too strong for the Lionesses on that occasion, showing their strength to dispatch England 3–0. More than 45,000 had watched the game, though, setting a new Lionesses record.

So much had changed in the five years that had passed in between. A few of the same players were still in the squad – Lucy, Steph, Jill and Jordan – but there were plenty more new faces. The women's game was changing too, now England's players were used to facing top sides in important matches, for club and country. England had become tougher opponents now and were ready to soak up any pressure the occasion would bring.

Germany, meanwhile, had a point to prove, after Sweden knocked them out of the World Cup in the last eight. That wasn't supposed to happen to a team ranked second in the world! Being eliminated in the quarter-finals matched their worst record at the tournament, leaving their fans frustrated. In France, they had had plenty of quality players to call upon:

Dzsenifer Marozsán, a mercurial midfielder.

Alex Popp, a spectacular striker and captain.

Lena Oberdorf, a teenage sensation.

And all three were in the starting eleven at Wembley!

England, on the other hand, had hit a patch of poor form since their World Cup semi-final exit at the hands of the United States, losing three of their next five matches. The press were questioning whether Phil was the right man for the job and many of the fans agreed that his time was up.

Leah though put her faith in Phil. Just like her, he lived and breathed football and pushed his players to be the best that they could be. Now she just had to keep working hard and try to nail down a place in his starting line-up.

And the young defender got her wish! She would partner skipper Steph in central defence. Her Arsenal teammates Jordan and Beth were both starting too, while best friend Keira kept her Number 4 shirt.

Ready to roar on the two teams to victory, a record crowd of 77,768 packed out Wembley. A sea of flags, scarves and banners flowed across every stand, with the majority bearing the name of the mighty

Lionesses. These were the occasions that every player relished!

In the game's early stages though, England looked nervous. Their sloppy start saw them go a goal behind in the eighth minute. Germany's captain had sent a warning shot just minutes before, striking the bar with a powerful shot. This time she made sure it went in, when she stooped to produce a header that beat the diving Mary Earps in goal.

After that, England began to settle. Ellen scampered onto a pass into the box, but was brought down by German keeper Merle Frohms. Penalty!

This was England's best chance to level the scores. Up stepped Nikita Parris, but she fired straight down the middle at Frohms. The German players all ran to embrace their keeper.

Ellen wasn't giving up though, she was desperate to reward the fans. When her next chance came, just before half-time, the striker latched onto Keira's floated pass and finished first time brilliantly. Germany looked for the offside flag, but none was raised. There was no VAR for the friendly. England were back on level terms!

Leah and the Lionesses played on, but failed to create many clear-cut chances in the second half. Instead, Germany found the back of the net next, when Mary Earps spilled the ball and Lina Magull slid in to score. This time, the assistant's flag went up straightaway – offside!

Then heartbreak for England, Germany scored in the ninetieth minute, after fine work from Klara Bühl. The visitors had won it.

All England's toil and hard work would count for nothing.

Despite the loss, Ellen was voted player of the match, yet she couldn't hide her disappointment. 'It's a dream come true to play at Wembley for your country and score,' the striker said in a heartfelt TV interview. 'But we're really sorry we couldn't get the result.'

Leah had a feeling the fans would forgive her – Ellen had given every last drop of energy.

The loss left the Lionesses feeling sour. Germany had taught them a lesson in those final minutes – to keep on fighting until the referee had blown the whistle. Football was a game of fine margins – just one extra tackle, a shot fired a fraction of a second earlier, a fingertip save – moments like these often proved the difference between winning and losing. England would have to work even harder next time, so they wouldn't have to feel like this again.

CHAPTER 16

NOISY NEIGHBOURS

After the international break, it was back to the bread and butter of the Women's Super League. Arsenal's first match back was one that had been circled in the Williamson family calendar back when the fixtures were first announced – they would play Tottenham Hotspur.

Tottenham's women's side had been promoted to the top league that season for the first time in their history, setting up the very first North London derby with neighbours Arsenal. If the teams could fuel even half the fierce rivalry between the men's sides, the fans were in for a cracker of a match!

For the new season, Spurs had brought in a whole

team of new players, including Arsenal's own Emma Mitchell on loan. The new signings would bring bags of experience to the Spurs' squad, but as a team, they hadn't had too long to gel.

Arsenal's squad on the other hand was packed with internationals – no fewer than ten players had competed at the World Cup that summer. What's more, in a pre-season friendly at Meadow Park, the Gunners had smashed Spurs 6–0. Spurs were clear second favourites – were they really expected to go toe-to-toe with Arsenal?

They did have something in their favour, though: the match would be played at the incredible new Tottenham Hotspur Stadium, home to the men's side. With its state-of-the-art facilities, enormous dressing rooms and even ice baths, the women were buzzing to play there. And while around a thousand fans filled their usual stadium, Brisbane Road, more than thirty times that number were expected that afternoon. *Incredible!*

Leah was thrilled that the World Cup had attracted so many new fans to the Women's Super League.

Long may it continue, she hoped.

As always, Leah had plenty of her own supporters coming to the match, but for once, they would be sitting at different ends of the ground. The North London derby was a serious business – she just hoped they would all still be friends after ninety minutes.

'Don't go making yourselves at home in our shiny new stadium now,' Dad joked on the morning of the match.

'Ha ha,' Leah laughed. 'One thing's for sure, our trophy room is bigger than yours!'

The truth was that any team would have been thrilled to play there every week, but at the moment playing at huge grounds, like the men did, was a distant dream for any women's side.

When the two teams walked out through the tunnel and into the sizeable stadium, the atmosphere was fizzing with electricity. The pristine pitch meanwhile was like a carpet – Leah half-expected someone to tell the players to take their boots off before stepping on it!

The teams formed their pre-match huddles at either

end.

'This game could be a banana skin, so let's stay focused,' Kim warned wisely. 'We don't want any slip-ups.'

'Let's make North London RED!' added Leah, fired up.

In the first half it was the home side who surprised, matching the league champions for skill and pace. Tottenham had definitely raised their game for the occasion. A good chance fell to Spurs' Kit Graham, but the forward shot straight at Arsenal's new Austrian keeper Manuela Zinsberger. They came close twice after that as half-time approached, flashing two shots wide as the home fans oohed and aahed.

After the interval though, Arsenal came out firing. Viv came closest to scoring on the hour, but saw her shot flick just past the post.

'We have to make this pressure count,' Kim blared at her teammates.

Whenever Arsenal found themselves in a tight spot, Kim was a player who always stepped up. The skipper opened the scoring at last with a perfectly placed left-footed drive from just inside the penalty box.

Gooooooooaaaaaaalllll!

Kim, Leah and the rest of the team sprinted straight over to celebrate with the noisy travelling fans.

Instantly, Leah knew that this was a memory that would stay with her for her whole life. *Special. Unforgettable.* She had never expected to play in a game like this in her career. Goosebumps prickled on her arms.

'The attendance today: 38,262. That's 38,262,' the Spurs stadium announcer boomed minutes later. 'Thank you all for your incredible support.'

Wow! That knocked the WSL record attendance out of the park! Whoever said no one cared about women's football was wrong.

A few minutes from time, Arsenal doubled their lead. When a Spurs defender made a sloppy back pass to Becky Spencer in goal, Viv (who else?) pounced to win the ball. She rounded the keeper and blasted her shot into the roof of the net. A quality finish!

It was the perfect moment for Arsenal fans to jump to their feet and serenade their Dutch striker:

Miedema is magic,
She's got two magic feet,
And when she weaves her magic spell
She's got defenders beat!
She mesmerises other teams
With her amazing magic run,
And when she sees the goal ahead
She's scoring just for fun!

Viv even treated them to a rare smile afterwards!

Then it was over. The bragging rights belonged to Arsenal!

What a day! Leah had happily soaked up every second.

'I grew up as an Arsenal fan, so nobody wants to lose these games,' Leah said in her interview. 'There's pride at stake and I loved being part of the occasion.'

Now to catch up with her family. Surely Dad had to expect a little teasing?

CHAPTER 17

AN OLYMPIC DREAM

From the age of two, when she began her very early gymnastics career, sport had always played a huge part in Leah's life. As a schoolgirl, she was one of those kids who did every sport she was offered – from gymnastics to athletics to football.

When London hosted the Olympics in 2012, it lit a fire in Leah. Then aged fifteen, she and her family were lucky enough to get tickets to watch the athletics in the London Stadium, built especially to host the Olympic and Paralympic events.

Memories of being in the Olympic Park for Super Saturday, the single greatest day in British Olympic history, would stay with Leah forever. Cheering her

Milton Keynes hometown hero Greg Rutherford to gold in the long jump was the highlight, while Jessica Ennis-Hill and Mo Farah both stormed to gold too. When the national anthem was played at each medal ceremony, Leah had to close her eyes to try to stem the tears.

Leah had always been a talented runner, both at cross country and in athletics. At one point she had seriously considered swapping her football boots for running spikes, but in the end, football won out. Becoming an Olympian was a target that always felt just that little bit further away.

At London 2012, Team GB had entered a women's football team for the first time, with a host of Arsenal heroes all representing Great Britain – Alex and Steph were in defence, Kim was in midfield, while Ellen, Kelly and Yanks joined the forward line. Leah and her Arsenal Academy teammates had always looked up to these Gunners greats, but now they were Olympians too. So cool!

The football associations of England, Scotland, Northern Ireland and Wales had also agreed that Team GB would field a team at the upcoming Tokyo 2020 games, made up of the best players from the four nations. When the news was announced, Leah felt a glimmer of hope. Maybe this could be her chance to become an Olympian, after all?

Although the games were still known as 'Tokyo 2020', they didn't take place until the summer of 2021, due to the COVID-19 pandemic. Even then, there were still strict rules in place that limited travel. England boss Phil Neville was expected to lead Team GB to Tokyo, but he left early after the Lionesses hit a slump in form.

Super coach Sarina Wiegman was set to take charge of England eventually, but not until she had taken her Netherlands team to the Olympics. In the meantime, Norwegian Hege Riise was hired to coach both England and Team GB.

Like Phil, Hege was a former player too, and had won a whole host of honours during a glittering career on the international stage – a World Cup, a Euros and an Olympic gold medal. She had once been crowned the best player in the world! Later on, Hege had helped coach the United States team.

With a small squad of eighteen players for the games,

Leah hoped Hege would choose her. She had completed another excellent season with Arsenal, but was never a player who took anything for granted. So, when the email arrived with good news, Leah was on cloud nine. Her Olympic dream was about to come true!

She knew her family would have made their way to Japan if they had been allowed, but sadly there would be no fans in any of the stadiums.

'We'd have only made each other cry!' Leah joked to Mum when she shared the news.

'Well, there will be tears from across the ocean,' Mum replied proudly. 'Guaranteed!'

Alongside Leah, Arsenal captain Kim had been chosen too, while their teammate Lotte Wubben-Moy was a reserve. But when Leah looked for Beth and Jordan's names on the list, they weren't even on standby for Tokyo.

Leah was devastated for her teammates and called them straightaway. Jordan seemed okay – albeit gutted – but being left out had hit Beth harder.

'I can't believe you're not coming,' Leah said to Beth. The sadness in her voice was clear.

'I can't either,' Beth sniffed, equally sadly. 'Make sure you win us a medal. I want to hear all about it when you get back.'

Going for gold was definitely the plan, Leah told herself.

*

Even without any fans to cheer them on, Team GB kicked off their Olympic competition with a comfortable 2–0 win over Chile. Ellen still brought out her famous 'goggles' goal celebration for everyone back home though, after scoring in each half. Steph and Millie Bright were Hege's chosen defensive duo, but Leah replaced Millie in the next match against hosts Japan.

Ellen sniffed out the game's only goal in an eerily empty Sapporo Dome. Leah was happy to have made her Olympic debut, and had made a crucial save towards the end. She would have put her foot through a brick wall to keep the ball out if she'd needed to.

With two wins from two games, Team GB were through to the quarter-finals. Their next opponents Canada, though, might be able to overtake them at the top of the table with a win. Hege switched her side up again, this time with Leah and Millie shoring up the defence.

Team GB scuffed first-half chances before an unmarked Adriana Leon netted for Canada to open the scoring. Frustrated, Leah picked the ball out of the back of the net. It was poor defending. They had to do better.

Scot Caroline Weir was unlucky not to score when her angled shot hit the bar and then the post, but her luck changed when a late effort went in taking a huge deflection on its way. 1–1!

'Yes, Caz!' Leah shouted, punching the air in relief. Staying unbeaten would give them confidence for the quarters.

For the match against Australia, Hege chose her strongest line-up, which included Leah! It was a huge honour. Team GB's defence began shakily though, letting in Aussie Alanna Kennedy to score. Then Ellen turned the game on its head, scoring two fine goals. She was playing out of her skin this tournament, putting the 'Great' into Great Britain.

But with a minute to go, Australia's own superstar

striker Sam Kerr equalised.

'We go again!' called Leah, seeing British heads begin to drop.

A frantic thirty minutes of extra time went by in a blur:

Team GB missed a penalty. Still 2–2.

Eighteen-year-old Mary Fowler scored for Australia. 2–3.

Sam Kerr rose above Steph to score her second goal. 2–4.

Ellen completed her hat-trick. 3–4.

Extra time ended. Team GB were out.

When she saw the tears streaming down Ellen's face, Leah's eyes filled up too. Together, Team GB had given everything, but they had fallen agonisingly short.

'You've been brilliant,' Hege told the young defender. 'One of our best players.'

Going out in extra time left a bitter taste, but Leah would bounce back from this defeat. And at the next big tournament, she would lead England all the way to victory.

CHAPTER 18

CAPTAIN MATERIAL

Fresh from the Olympics, Dutch coach Sarina Wiegman arrived at last to take the reins of the England team. She had plenty of work ahead of her and not much time to do it; she had to get to know all the players and prepare the Lionesses for two important World Cup qualifiers that month. North Macedonia and Luxembourg would be their next opponents.

Sarina's arrival had created a buzz of excitement in the camp. This was a coach who had won the Euros and taken her Netherlands side to a World Cup final too. Now she was tasked with taking England on that same journey.

Leah had loved the first couple of training sessions with Sarina. The Dutch coach was easy to talk to and she listened to the players' ideas too. Tactics were tweaked and the squad seemed to have gone up a gear already, with everyone keen to make a good impression.

Who would make the starting line-up? What formation would they play? And, with Ellie Roebuck out injured, who would get the goalkeeper jersey? These were just some of the dilemmas yet to be solved.

The night before the North Macedonia match, England had travelled down to their team hotel in Southampton. The players were eating dinner together when Sarina came over to Leah's table.

'Come and find me when you've finished,' said Sarina, putting a hand on Leah's shoulder.

The girls at the table shared a sideways glance.

'Will do,' Leah replied, trying to stop her cheeks from flushing pink. *Uh-oh. What have I done?* she began to panic.

But when she sat down with Sarina, the coach had

a pleasant surprise in store for her.

'How would you like to be captain tomorrow?' Sarina asked.

Leah laughed and breathed out a huge sigh of relief. 'I thought I was in trouble!' she said.

Quite the opposite! Earlier that day, Steph had picked up an injury in their training session that would sadly rule her out of the match. The England captain had returned to her club, Manchester City, Sarina explained. Now the Lionesses needed a skipper to fill in and Leah's name was the first on Sarina's list.

Wow! thought Leah. She was nowhere near as experienced as Ellen or even Millie. And while Leah had captained the Young Lionesses through the age groups, she never expected to captain the senior side at the age of twenty-four. *The captain's armband finds you*, she always told herself. *Not the other way around.*

'Yes, please!' she replied quickly, before Sarina had the chance to change her mind.

The girls in the dressing room respected Leah and she felt ready to take on more responsibility, on the pitch and in front of the media too. Her main concern – silly, she knew – was whether the captain's armband would fit her. *My arms are so skinny!* she worried.

The first phone calls she made were to her family; she was desperate to share her incredible news. She knew her mum, dad and gran would be overflowing with pride.

Mum's screams were so loud that Leah had to hold the phone away from her ear. 'We'll all be there, of course,' Mum promised.

Leah's England teammates were also right behind her from the start. They loved her passion for the game, and her honesty and kindness too.

Leah was always proud to represent her country, but the next night in Southampton felt more special still. Even if it was just for these next two games, captaining the Lionesses would be the ultimate honour of her life.

Leah could feel it was going to be a fantastic night under the lights, as she led England out at St Mary's Stadium. Sarina was playing her in central midfield, so she could expect to see plenty of the ball.

Ranked outside the top one hundred nations, North Macedonia weren't expected to trouble England, but the home side couldn't afford any slip-ups.

'Let's stay calm and show what we can do,' the new skipper told her team.

England burst out of the blocks, creating some good early chances, before Leah stroked a fine pass forwards to Ella Toone. Ella ran onto it and rolled the ball under the keeper's body to score on her full debut. *Gooooooaaaaallll!*

It wasn't until just before the break that England scored again, Ellen firing home from ten yards out. The striker was involved again a couple of minutes later, as a mix-up in the North Macedonian defence led to an unfortunate own goal.

Midway through the second half, Leah was fouled in the box. England had been in search of a new penalty-taker for a while now and Ellen passed the audition! 4–0.

Goals five, six and seven followed in quick succession before Beth added a brilliant eighth goal on ninety minutes. Leah was so glad Sarina had brought Beth back for England; she made such a fierce Lioness.

The score was 8–0! It was the perfect start for Sarina as coach and Leah as captain. They had achieved what they set out to do:

✓ Score lots of goals.

✓ Keep a clean sheet.

✓ Make the fans proud.

Despite scoring eight though, England had wasted plenty more chances in front of goal.

It should definitely have been double figures, Leah admitted to herself.

Still, they had the chance to do better in just a few days' time. Like North Macedonia, Luxembourg were also way down in the world rankings.

England were 4–0 up by half-time, Mary Earps in goal hadn't touched the ball once. As the game reached ninety minutes, their score had increased to 7–0. Luxembourg just didn't have the quality to compete with the Lionesses.

Leah glanced over to the sidelines, to see a frown

on Sarina's face. This manager demanded the very best. If England created ten chances, then they should score all ten.

'Come on, girls,' Leah said, clapping her hands. 'Let's keep pushing until the final whistle.'

And her teammates listened, taking advantage of tired Luxembourg legs to score their eighth, ninth and tenth goals before the ref blew for full time. Much better!

Two easy games, but one thing was clear – Leah made an excellent captain.

CHAPTER 19

THE ARNOLD CLARK CUP

With Sarina as boss and Leah as captain, the future for England was looking bright. Steph's injury was worse than the physios thought, so Leah kept the armband for England's next World Cup qualifiers that autumn.

Leah had played for England at Wembley before, but going back there as captain against Northern Ireland was a special night. And when her teammate Beth became the first Lioness to score a hat-trick in the famous stadium, the night became more memorable still.

In the very next match, Leah scored her first competitive goal for England, as the team hit double figures again, 0–10, away in Latvia.

But just as Leah was in the form of her life, she was forced to hobble off the pitch against Spurs. This time, a troublesome hamstring injury would keep her out for six weeks.

Leah was sad to miss the next matches with England – particularly when they faced Latvia at home, and this time scored a 20–0 record victory – but was thankful that the injury hadn't happened six months later. Missing the Euros would have been her worst nightmare.

Since the Olympics, Leah felt like she had been on a treadmill, playing matches all over Europe for club and country. In the end, her body had told her it needed a rest. Now Leah would take some time out over Christmas and come back stronger in the new year.

*

While Leah was fit again to play in the Arnold Clark Cup in February 2022, Steph was still sidelined following surgery on her Achilles. It meant that Leah would captain the Lionesses in a tournament. This time, England knew the games would be much trickier: they faced three of the world's top ten teams over the week – Canada, Spain and Germany.

Under Sarina though, England were stronger and more competitive. They didn't fear anyone.

'We're going into this tournament to win it. It's perfect preparation for the summer,' Leah told the press, feeling positive.

The first match was in Middlesbrough, against Bev Priestman's Canada. Bev had once been Phil's assistant coach, so knew the Lionesses' strengths and weaknesses well. Sarina welcomed the test against a top opponent; six months earlier, Canada had won Olympic gold.

In the opening twenty minutes, the action was end to end. Canada almost scored from a corner, with Leah caught napping. It was the wake-up call she needed – Leah went on the attack next and fired just wide from outside the box. Close!

Then when Canada failed to clear a corner, the ball dropped perfectly for Millie to volley home a screamer. What a goal!

'Defenders aren't supposed to be able to do that!'

Leah joked.

Unfortunately for England, Canada had quality players in their side too; after fifty-six minutes Janine Beckie scored a stunning equaliser. Leah left the field soon after, as Sarina brought on some strong subs. The Lionesses could have won it late on, but a penalty appeal in stoppage time was turned down. Canada and England shared the spoils.

Next, in Norwich, England faced Spain, a dangerous side with matchwinners in most positions – not least the world's best player, midfielder Alexia Putellas. Sarina brought fresh legs into the starting line-up, so everyone had a chance to shine. Leah started on the bench, but replaced Jill Scott with about half an hour to play. And before the teams knew it, the ninety minutes were up. Neither side had managed to score, but the Carrow Road crowd had been more than entertained.

England's final fixture, in Wolverhampton, was against old rivals Germany. Leah thought back to the last time the sides had met; Germany had just edged the win in a brilliant battle at a packed Wembley. Now the Lionesses were hungry for revenge.

Earlier the same day, Spain had beaten Canada, which meant that England would have to win well if they wanted to claim the trophy. There was just one problem – England had never beaten Germany on home soil before.

But Leah wasn't going to let a small detail like that stop her side. She gathered the players into a pre-match huddle. 'Come on, girls,' she urged. 'We've got to make that trophy ours.'

The Arnold Clark Cup wasn't the biggest prize England pursued that year, but winning it would send a message to the rest of Europe and keep the Lionesses' unbeaten run under Sarina going.

A strong eleven started the match, with Leah back in midfield. This team had the belief – together they could beat anyone. Ellen struck first, but Germany's Lina Magull levelled with a quality free kick four minutes before the break.

A draw wouldn't be enough to win the trophy though, England had to score again. On eighty minutes, Leah tried her luck, unleashing a shot that fizzed over the bar.

'We can do this, *keep going!*' she roared to her teammates.

And while in the past, England might have hoped they would score again, this time the whole team believed they really would. As the minutes ticked down, Millie pushed up the pitch, in the role of makeshift striker. When the ball bounced back to her in the box following some brilliant work by Lauren Hemp, there was Millie to slot home. Boom!

It was well into added time when the little magician Fran Kirby pulled out her final trick. After tearing down the pitch from inside her own half, she delivered a superb finish. 3–1! A stunning solo goal. England had just pipped Spain to win the very first Arnold Clark Cup!

Soon after, the team collected their winners' medals and Leah raised the silver trophy.

'Yessssssssssss!' the girls all cheered as one as streamers showered down.

After the match, Leah spoke proudly about her team. 'On days like today you learn how to win, even when things aren't going your way,' she said in her interview.

England hadn't been at their best, but together they had found a way to grind out the win. Thankfully, the lesson had been learned before the biggest tournament of their lives.

CHAPTER 20

LEADING THE LIONESSES

In her new role as captain, Leah had proved to be a great leader, on and off the pitch. Her fellow Lionesses loved her and whether they had one cap or one hundred caps, Leah made sure that everyone knew they were an important part of the team.

So, when Sarina made Leah the captain for good that spring, the Arsenal hero was beyond proud. She wasn't sure whether the feeling would ever sink in. It was the biggest honour of her life to follow in the footsteps of all the special names who had worn the armband before her. She couldn't wait for the summer and the home Women's Euros – and now all she had to do was stay fit.

In what felt like the blink of an eye, the tournament arrived. The thirteenth Women's European Championship. Sixteen teams. Ten stadiums. And hundreds of thousands of fans. With home crowds behind them, England would never have a better chance to battle for the trophy. If everything went their way, this team of talented Lionesses could make history and change the game for women's football.

Old Trafford in Manchester hosted England's opener, with a boisterous crowd of more than 68,000 fans expecting all three points against Austria. Whether it was the noise or just nerves, England were not at their best, but they did do enough to score. In the end, Beth's dink over the keeper after sixteen minutes proved the matchwinner.

'We've got the win, that's all that matters,' Leah said calmly, after the match.

Next the Lionesses travelled to Brighton. Norway were stronger opponents on paper than Austria, but that night England ripped up the rule book. Their attackers were on fire, and ensured they were 3–0 up before half an hour had been played. After that,

Norway crumbled in a match that would go down in history. It ended England 8, Norway 0. England were in dreamland!

It was the biggest score ever in a Women's Euros match. Five different Lionesses had scored. Beth had netted an incredible hat-trick, earning a kiss on the forehead from Leah!

The Lionesses wrapped up the group stage with another high-scoring game, this time against home nations rivals Northern Ireland. Their 5–0 victory saw England easily top their group. Nine points earned, fourteen goals scored and not a single goal conceded!

So far, so good, but England had drawn Spain for their quarter-final back in Brighton. Many had tipped Spain for the title, but they had lost their best player Alexia Putellas to a bad knee injury before a ball had been kicked at the Euros. How would La Roja fare without her?

A tense first half ended goalless, but with Spain dominating possession. England had come closest to taking the lead when Ellen's strike was ruled out for offside. If another chance to score came up, they had to put it away.

It was Spain however who scored first, Esther González stroking the ball past Mary Earps. The Brighton crowd was suddenly silent – England had to score or their Euros dream would be over. It was their first setback in the competition; now the Lionesses had to bounce back.

Never once did it cross Leah's mind that England were going out, they had plenty of players who could create a goal out of nothing, and more than enough time left to do so.

'Let's keep going, girls,' the skipper shouted. 'We've got this.'

On came Alessia Russo and Chloe Kelly to replace top scorer Beth and record scorer Ellen. The young attackers would add energy, but this would be the biggest game they had ever played in. Rachel Daly shot Leah a worried look.

'The boss knows what she's doing,' Leah said confidently. 'Trust in Sarina!'

The second half continued in a frenzy. A penalty appeal for England was turned down. A dipping shot was saved by Mary Earps. Time was running out.

Then six minutes before full time, super sub Ella Toone volleyed home the equaliser. A scruffy goal from five yards out, it was worth its weight in gold. After the goal, the momentum switched England's way. Could they make it count in extra time?

Georgia Stanway certainly could! Picking up the ball in midfield, she drove on towards the box. With tired Spanish legs backing off, Georgia fired a thunderbolt past Sandra Paños.

Goooooaaaaalllll!

The crowd roared louder than at any point that night. At last the mood switched from despair to delight.

'It's coming home, It's coming home . . .' the England fans broke into song.

Incredible!

Eventually, after 124 gruelling minutes, England were through. Sarina led the celebrations pumping both fists in the air, while the players hugged and danced before the crowd.

In her TV interview, Leah spoke of a special

performance. England had shown their resilience and proved they could overcome any test that stood in their way.

'I'm so proud of these girls!' she gushed. She was just sorry that extra time had kept the nation up so late!

Soon, just four teams remained in the semi-finals. England, Sweden, Germany and France. England would play Sweden in Sheffield, while Germany were drawn against France.

It was another full house at Bramall Lane when England faced the Olympic silver medallists. As Europe's highest-ranked team, Sweden were looking to spoil England's party. Both teams burst out of the blocks, with Leah's Arsenal teammate Stina Blackstenius hitting the woodwork before ten minutes had passed. Leah wasn't about to let that happen again!

England played on, trusting in their tactics. Then after thirty-four minutes, Beth blasted her side into the lead with a brilliant swivel and first-time shot. And just after half time, Beth added an assist, picking out

Lucy at the far post from a corner to make it two.

Alessia was so keen to get on the scoresheet next that she attempted a ridiculous shot. Facing the wrong away, her only option was to backheel the ball towards goal. Her shot rolled into the back of the net having nutmegged a defender and the keeper in one fell swoop! 3–0.

'There are no words!' gasped Leah, throwing her arms around the young striker.

And when Fran's delicious chip beat Hedvig Lindahl from outside the box, the Swedish keeper could have been forgiven for thinking about hanging up her gloves.

'England are going to Wembley!' the commentator blared.

CHAPTER 21

THAT FINAL

And we all know what happened next . . .

Two teams.

Wembley Stadium.

87,192 fans.

One hundred and twenty minutes.

One goal to Germany.

Two to England!

And the very first European trophy for the Lionesses.

Leah had played every single minute of the tournament, including extra time in the final two rounds against Spain and Germany. Now it was over, her legs felt like jelly.

The players lined up excitedly to collect their medals

before taking their places on the podium. Then Leah was handed the beautiful glass-and-silver trophy, freshly engraved with the name of the new champions: ENGLAND. It was love at first sight.

This one is special, thought Leah, as she carried it like a baby towards her teammates. *Heavy too!*

'Give us a hand here,' Leah told Millie with a wink.

'Happy to help!' her vice-captain replied, smiling.

Of course, it wasn't really that heavy, Leah was just being kind, wanting to share the once-in-a-lifetime moment. *Standard for Leah*, Millie thought to herself.

So Leah and Millie hoisted the trophy together, while confetti rained down and fireworks fizzed. Everything about that moment was perfect. Her amazing teammates and coaches, the incredible fans and all her family in the crowd; Leah wouldn't have changed a thing.

Then came the music, the dancing and the victory laps, the players draped in St George flags, waving scarves above their heads. The Lionesses never wanted to leave that pitch.

And when the TV cameras caught up with the

captain for a quick interview at last, Leah spoke from the heart.

'We've finally done it, we've finally brought everyone together,' she said passionately. 'The legacy of this team is as winners and I'm so proud to be English!'

After a fifty-six year wait for a trophy, Leah and the Lionesses had brought football home at last.

The celebrations would continue long into the night, like no party Leah had ever known before. Lucy leading a conga of gatecrashers into Sarina's press conference was one of the highlights! The players' rowdy rendition of 'Three Lions' with Mary and Lucy dancing on the desks had their Dutch coach barely believing her eyes.

*

The following day the Lionesses headed to Trafalgar Square for a very special after-party. No one had had much sleep, but the players were still raring to celebrate with the fans.

At times like these Leah wished she drank coffee like the other girls, but she had only ever liked hot chocolate. A boring ham sandwich was her pre-match staple too – her teammates always teased her for that one.

Luckily, her taste in music was more adventurous, Leah played everything from to dance to rap to country in her role of team DJ. She loved introducing the girls to random songs from every era. She was always in charge of the playlist on the coach journey. It was her job to make sure that the party carried on all the way into town.

A stage had been hastily built in front of Nelson's Column looking out on to Trafalgar Square, where 7,000 fans were waiting in the sunshine to welcome the new champions.

Just wow! thought Leah, as she looked out across a sea of St George flags waving proudly. The Lionesses felt like rock stars!

On the stage, Leah's old Arsenal buddy Alex Scott was ready to greet the team. 'Please welcome to the stage your victorious England Lionesses, everyone!'

Then came a whirlwind concert of speeches, songs and dancing. Through it all, the grin never left Leah's face.

CHAPTER 22

THE EUROS EFFECT

As Leah had always said, although she wore the captain's armband, there were loads of strong leaders in that squad. Players willing to stand up and be counted when it came to pushing women's football on.

On the coach home from Trafalgar Square, Arsenal teammates Leah, Beth and Lotte Wubben-Moy were chatting about an idea that Lotte had been thinking about. Now that the Lionesses were European Champions, they had been given a precious opportunity to make their voice heard. They all felt a responsibility to help give girls the same access as boys to play football, just as the generations before them had tried to do. They didn't want girls to have to cut their hair or get called names just because they wanted to play the sport they loved. It just wasn't fair.

'We'll use our platform and write a public letter demanding that all girls are allowed to play football at school,' Lotte said.

Hardly any of the Lionesses had been able to play football in PE lessons growing up, while for boys in their classes it was much easier. Girls had had to set up their own teams, often having to travel miles to play. That required time and money, which not every family had. And in 2022, the same problems still affected girls up and down the country.

'That's an excellent idea,' said Beth.

'We have to make this happen,' added Leah.

The Lionesses got off the coach feeling fired up about the future, but they were fast running out of energy. No sleep and nothing to eat was not a good combination! Leah and Beth hoped they would be forgiven for a fast-food takeaway, just this once.

Lotte drafted the letter the next day. At that time, two politicians – Liz Truss and Rishi Sunak – were going head-to-head in the battle to becoming the next prime minister of the United Kingdom, so Lotte addressed the letter to them both. All twenty-three Lionesses added their signatures, united in their message.

Word spread quickly on TV, in the newspapers and on social media too, gaining support far and wide. At last, girls' sport was being taken seriously. By the following spring, the UK government had pledged £600 million to create equal sporting opportunities for girls in schools.

Leah hoped that the money would open doors for all the young girls that the Lionesses had inspired to pick up a football. It was a great result, but there was plenty more that the team could do to have a positive impact on society. The Lionesses wanted to create a legacy of changing things for the better.

*

In the days after the Euros final, all Leah wanted to do was to relax with her family back in Newport Pagnell. Sarina's squad had been bubble-wrapped for the tournament to keep them grounded, so it was nice to hear all about what had really been going on in the country and how the Lionesses' performances had brought people together over the past few weeks.

Overnight, a mural had appeared in Newport Pagnell that summed up the town's pride for one of their own. On one wall was painted a portrait of Leah against the St George flag, while a second wall showed Leah wearing her Euros medal with a lioness in the background.

'Wait until you see it,' Amanda told her daughter. 'You're going to love it.'

Leah couldn't go just yet, though, she was likely to get mobbed!

Then it was time for a little getaway on the Spanish island of Ibiza. Leah headed to Stansted Airport disguised in a baseball cap and sunglasses. On arrival at the terminal, she joined the queue as normal for her budget flight to Spain.

Even if winning the Euros had made her a millionaire overnight, she wasn't the type to be suddenly demanding private jets. Leah was Leah. Daughter, sister, football fan. Wherever this journey and her new-found fame with the Lionesses took her, she never wanted to change who she was.

But when the plane landed, her secret was out. A small crowd of people all wanted to congratulate the England captain or ask for a picture. Life might never be the same again, she realised.

CHAPTER 23

WORLD CUP HEARTACHE

It had been just over a month since that incredible final at Wembley, but when the Lionesses met up for their next camp, it felt like no time had passed at all. Catching up with the squad felt so good, but two familiar faces were missing. Ellen and Jill had decided to go out on a high and hang up their boots; the Euros final was the last match of their careers.

Football was a sport that didn't stand still for long though; now the Lionesses had another important match in their very next game. Beat Austria away, and England would qualify for the World Cup with a game to spare. They had had been flawless in qualification so far, taking maximum points in their nine games. Seventy-eight goals scored and zero conceded. It didn't get much better than that!

Goals from Alessia and Nikita Parris sealed the win and, with it, England's place at the tournament in Australia and New Zealand the following year. This time, there were no wild celebrations nor any great fanfare. It was job done. Leah led the applause for the travelling England fans.

A few days later, the Lionesses scored a perfect ten against Luxembourg, but a foot injury meant it was game over for England's skipper by half time. 'Not again,' she groaned.

On her return to London, the injury was revealed to be worse than she thought. She had played more matches than ever in 2022, and tiredness had finally taken its toll on her body.

In the end, Leah missed two months of action with Arsenal and England. As well as some of the Gunners' important games, she had to sit out England's next match at Wembley against world champions the United States.

It was never easy watching when she was injured,

but Leah found it especially tough sitting in the buzzing Wembley stands that night. When her teammates walked out for the warm-up, her heart began to ache. Of all the highs and lows that year, this was definitely a low.

In an entertaining match, England ran out as 2–1 winners, thanks to goals from Lauren Hemp, Georgia Stanway and some helpful VAR decisions.

After that night, Leah kept her distance from the Lionesses squad. Missing out on the fun of the camps and buzz of the matches was just too painful. Some time away from the game gave her the space that she needed and, at last, there was light at the end of the tunnel. After two months out, Leah was back! Now she could look forward.

On her return to the WSL, Leah was rewarded with her two-hundredth appearance for Arsenal and a framed shirt with the Number 200. Reaching the milestone in her first match back from injury was just the boost she needed.

Before long, she was back for her beloved Lionesses too, pulling the strings in midfield at the second

Arnold Clark Cup in early 2023. Convincing wins against South Korea, Italy and Belgium saw England defend their trophy, with Leah scoring twice in their 6–1 win over Belgium. It felt brilliant to be back!

Another tournament, more silverware and the Lionesses' unbeaten run under Sarina now stretched to an incredible twenty-nine games. Could they make it thirty by beating South American champions Brazil in the Finalissima at Wembley? Yes! But this time it went to penalties after Brazil grabbed a very late equaliser to cancel out Ella Toone's opener for England. Mary Earps in goal and Chloe Kelly, the scorer of the final penalty, were the shoot-out heroes. Leah proudly lifted her fourth trophy as Lionesses captain.

'Each time I get to do this feels like the biggest honour of my life,' Leah said in the press conference after the match. Even though she was captain and one of the team's best players, she would never take the armband or her place in the team for granted. Her boots were firmly on the ground.

The media's questions about the World Cup that

summer had begun early. It was hard not to get excited about the tournament in Australia and New Zealand. At the 2019 World Cup in France, Leah had played just six minutes. Sure, England were Champions of Europe, but the best teams in the whole world would be hunting for glory Down Under. What's more, the Lionesses now had a target on their backs. Leah had seen it before: other teams would raise their games to try to beat them.

We wouldn't want it any other way, she smiled to herself.

Unfortunately, though, the universe had other plans for the England captain. It happened with fewer than one hundred days to go until the World Cup. Table-toppers Manchester United were hosting third-placed Arsenal at Leigh Sports Village when twelve minutes into the match, Leah went down in an ordinary-looking challenge. She signalled to the bench straightaway that something was wrong before being helped down the tunnel, clearly limping. Fans feared the worst.

A couple of days later, scans showed that Leah's

knee was badly damaged. An 'anterior cruciate ligament injury (ACL),' the doctors told her. She knew immediately what that meant. Beth and Viv had been on the treatment table for months now with the same injury, and were only about halfway through their rehab. There would be no Champions League semi-finals for Leah and no World Cup. As well as the pain in her knee, it felt like her heart had broken in two.

And while Leah knew she would eventually bounce back, this was the worst injury of her career. To not be able to help Arsenal challenge for the league title and the Champions League in the final weeks of the season felt almost unbearable. Having to sit out the World Cup with England at the peak of her career was equally as tough – the tournament only came around once every four years.

Now Leah needed surgery and time away from football to let the news sink in. She would need to stay mentally strong this next year, while she trusted her body to heal. She knew she may never find out what had caused the injury exactly. Too many matches? Poor quality pitches? Football boots not designed for women's feet? Or perhaps all of these things. But one thing she felt certain of was that she wasn't alone.

Beth and Viv would be with her all the way and all her friends and family too.

'You don't have to ask,' said Beth. 'We've got you. Every step.'

So after a little while, Leah dried her tears and put her game-face on. She was ready to tackle this injury and kick it into touch.

And whether it was from the stands or further afar, Leah would be there through thick and thin for all her teammates, as Arsenal and England's biggest supporter.

Arsenal

- Women's FA Cup: 2013–14, 2015–16
- Women's League Cup: 2015, 2017–18, 2022–23
- Women's Super League: 2018–19

England

- SheBelieves Cup: 2019
- UEFA Women's Championship: 2022
- Arnold Clark Cup: 2022, 2023
- Finalissima: 2023

Individual

- England Women's Youth Player of the Year: 2014
- FA WSL Continental Cup Player of the Year: 2014
- PFA Young Women's Player of the Year: 2015
- FA WSL PFA Team of the Year: 2019–20, 2021–22
- UEFA Women's Championship Team of the Tournament: 2022
- IFFHS Women's World Team: 2022
- FIFA FIFPRO Women's World 11: 2022

WILLIAMSON

6 THE FACTS

NAME: Leah Cathrine Williamson

DATE OF BIRTH: 29 March 1997

PLACE OF BIRTH: Milton Keynes, Buckinghamshire

NATIONALITY: English

BEST FRIEND: Keira Walsh

CURRENT CLUB: Arsenal

POSITION: Central defender/midfielder

THE STATS	
Height (cm):	170
Club appearances:	133
Club goals:	8
Club trophies:	5
International appearances:	42
International goals:	4
International trophies:	5
Ballon d'Ors:	0

★★★ HERO RATING: 97 ★★★

GREATEST MOMENTS

14 JULY 2014
MILLWALL LIONESSES 0–4 ARSENAL

Teenage Leah got off the mark for Arsenal, scoring a fantastic goal. When the ball landed at her feet, she turned between two defenders and delivered a devastating strike. In a team of legends, Leah proved she deserved to be there.

14 MAY 2016
ARSENAL 1–0 CHELSEA

Playing at Wembley was too big to dream about while Leah was growing up – and it was unimaginable in the women's game. So, when Arsenal beat Chelsea through a Danielle Carter classic in front of 32,912 fans at the famous stadium, Leah was on cloud nine! Arsenal won the FA Cup for a record fourteenth time.

4 SEPTEMBER 2018
KAZAKHSTAN 0–6 ENGLAND

Leah's first start for England came away in Kazakhstan. A team of young Lionesses, hungry to go to the World Cup, scored six times, with Leah playing the full ninety minutes in midfield.

17 NOVEMBER 2019
TOTTENHAM HOTSPUR 0–2 ARSENAL

The first ever North London derby at Spurs' slick new stadium was a day to remember. The WSL crowd record was smashed, with 38,262 fans cheering on the teams. Arsenal soon silenced the home crowd with goals from Kim and Viv. North London was red!

31 JULY 2022
ENGLAND 2–1 GERMANY

Beating Germany at Wembley in front of 87,192 fans to win the Women's Euro is a day that will live with Leah and the Lionesses forever. The nail-biting game went to extra time, before Chloe Kelly sealed their historic win and Leah lifted the trophy!

TEST YOUR KNOWLEDGE

QUESTIONS

1. What is Leah's squad number for Arsenal?

2. Who are Arsenal's North London rivals?

3. How old was Leah when she joined Arsenal's Academy?

4. What is the name of Leah's little brother?

5. Which coach gave Leah her senior England debut?

6. Which team did Arsenal beat in the final when Leah won her first FA Cup?

7. In which country did Leah play for Team GB at an Olympic Games?

8. In which other sport might Leah have been an Olympian?

9. In which season did Leah win her first league title with the Gunners?

10. How old was Leah when she first captained England's senior Lionesses?

11. Who is Leah's best friend in the England team?

Answers below . . . No cheating!

1. *Number 6.* **2.** *Tottenham Hotspur.* **3.** *Nine.* **4.** *Jacob.* **5.** *Phil Neville.* **6.** *Everton.* **7.** *Tokyo.* **8.** *Athletics.* **9.** *2018–19.* **10.** *Twenty-four.* **11.** *Keira Walsh.*

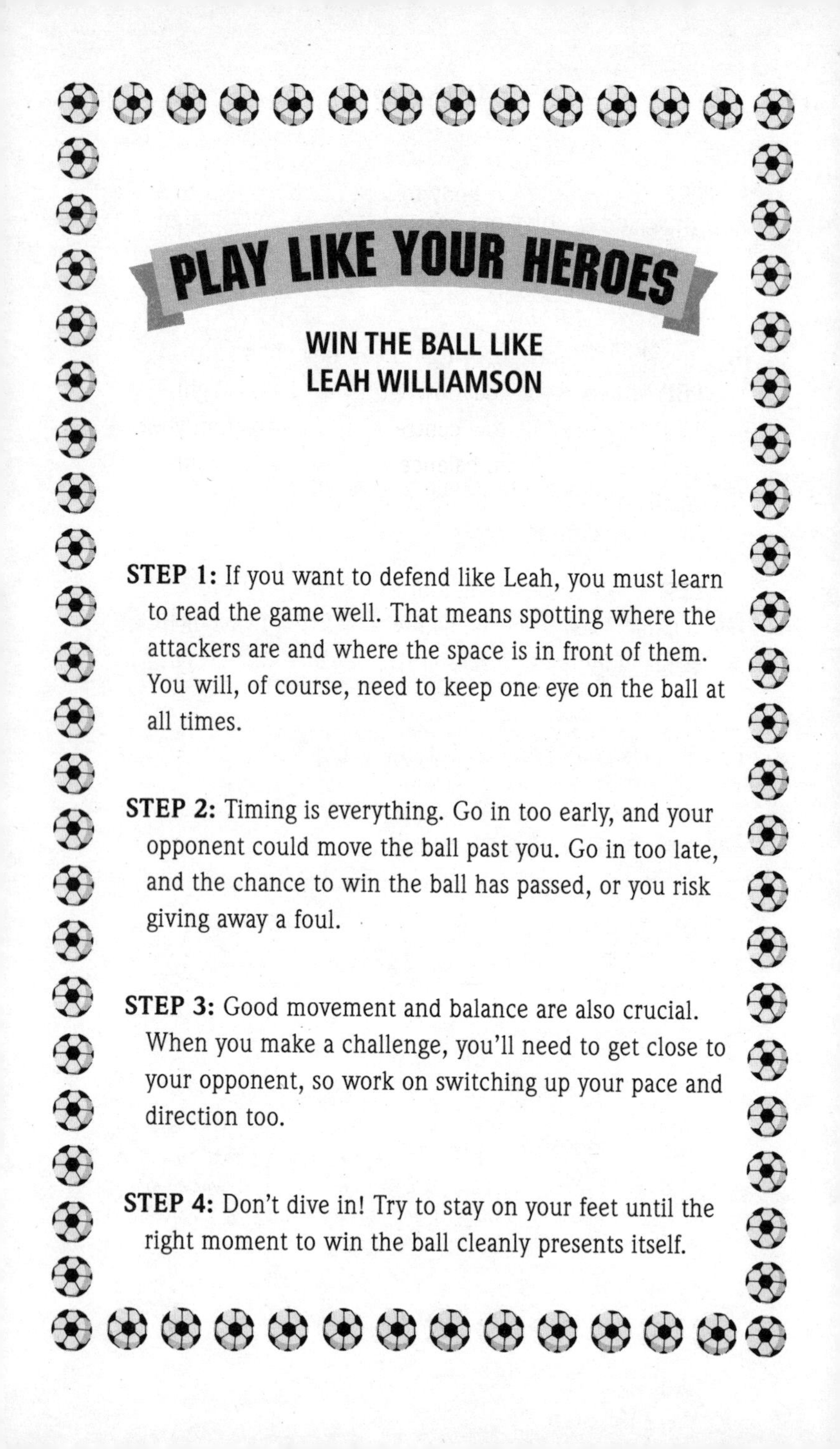

PLAY LIKE YOUR HEROES

WIN THE BALL LIKE LEAH WILLIAMSON

STEP 1: If you want to defend like Leah, you must learn to read the game well. That means spotting where the attackers are and where the space is in front of them. You will, of course, need to keep one eye on the ball at all times.

STEP 2: Timing is everything. Go in too early, and your opponent could move the ball past you. Go in too late, and the chance to win the ball has passed, or you risk giving away a foul.

STEP 3: Good movement and balance are also crucial. When you make a challenge, you'll need to get close to your opponent, so work on switching up your pace and direction too.

STEP 4: Don't dive in! Try to stay on your feet until the right moment to win the ball cleanly presents itself.

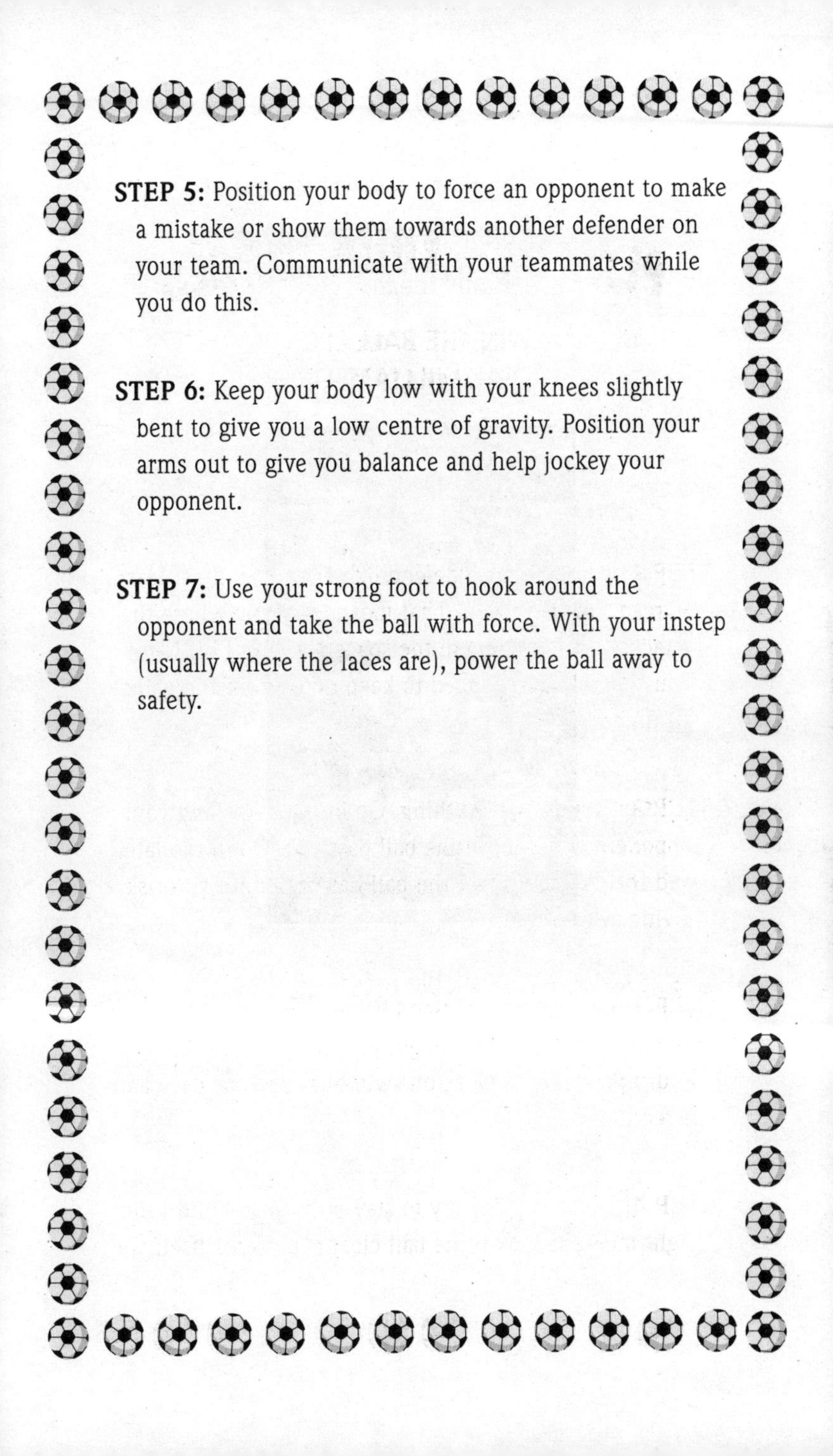

STEP 5: Position your body to force an opponent to make a mistake or show them towards another defender on your team. Communicate with your teammates while you do this.

STEP 6: Keep your body low with your knees slightly bent to give you a low centre of gravity. Position your arms out to give you balance and help jockey your opponent.

STEP 7: Use your strong foot to hook around the opponent and take the ball with force. With your instep (usually where the laces are), power the ball away to safety.

Turn the page for a sneak preview of another brilliant football story by Emily Stead. . .

MEAD

Available now!

CHAPTER 1

A NIGHT TO REMEMBER

6 July 2022, Old Trafford, Manchester
Women's Euro 2022 Group A match –
England vs Austria

At last, the wait was over. The thirteenth Women's European Championship – and biggest ever – was greeted by a fanfare of music and fireworks. Sixteen teams. Ten stadiums. And hundreds of thousands of fans.

With home crowds on England's side, the Lionesses would never have a better chance of winning the trophy. It was the biggest summer of their lives – one that could see their hearts broken or see them hailed as heroes. Whatever happened, their goal was to make the nation proud.

England's first opponents were Austria. Just a few months earlier, the two sides had met in a World Cup qualifier in Sunderland. It was a special night for forward Beth Mead, returning to the city where she'd first made her name as a teenage goalscoring sensation. She had so wanted to impress at the Stadium of Light, and thought she had won a penalty that could double England's lead, only to see the ref wave 'play on'. Maybe she'd have more luck in Manchester?

Old Trafford had been chosen to kick off the Women's Euros – the 'Theatre of Dreams', the fans called it. As Beth looked around the packed stadium, memories of her first visit there as a young girl came flooding back. She'd travelled there with her dad, Richard, to see her hero David Beckham in action for Manchester United. She remembered their seats were really high up, with lots of concrete steps for little legs to climb, but it was worth it when they reached the top of the family stand. Beth spotted the Number 7 straightaway on the enormous grass pitch below, running his hands through his floppy blond hair.

Now Beth had the chance to become a hero too, as part of a squad of twenty-three talented Lionesses. They could make history if they won the Women's Euros, their first major trophy.

Five teams had a good chance of winning – Spain, Sweden, France and Germany were all dangerous sides – but England's home advantage made them favourites. The tag of favourites usually brought with it a huge weight of expectation, but England's special coach Sarina Wiegman had a way of somehow soaking up all the pressure for them.

She knew what it took to win the trophy, winning the Euros the last time around with her native Netherlands.

England's players trusted her completely. 'If we work together and try our best, success should follow,' Sarina told her team.

Old Trafford had a carnival vibe, with flags waving, music blasting out through the stadium sound system and the fans in full voice. A Mexican wave rippled around the ground before the game had even kicked off! While the two teams warmed up, Beth blocked out the noise. She was purely focused on the game ahead.

And after sixteen minutes it was Beth who gave England a dream start. Fran Kirby spotted Beth's darting run into the box and lifted a clever pass over the Austria defence towards her. Beth controlled the pass on her chest with a perfect first touch, before dinking the ball over the keeper. Then suddenly it felt like time eased into slow motion. An Austrian defender lunged desperately to try to make a save, but the ball crashed up onto the crossbar.

Had it crossed the line? It was tight, but Beth was sure it had. She reeled away to celebrate with the fans. The keeper, Beth's Arsenal teammate Manuela Zinsberger, wasn't protesting. Still, the goal would be checked by the Video Assistant Referee.

Time dragged slower still until finally, *GOAL!* the screens around the stadium flashed.

'That was cold!' said Georgia Stanway, the first to

smother Beth in a happy embrace.

Beth hugged her back, grinning. Inside though, she felt far from cool. That made it fifteen goals in her last fifteen games. She was a player on fire!

The crowd thought so too, as they burst into song:

'Beth Mead's on fire,
Your defence is terrified . . .'

Once they had the lead, England found their rhythm, and pushed Austria deeper and deeper.

Midway through the second half, high-fives were exchanged as Fran, Ellen White and Beth were replaced by Ella Toone, Alessia Russo and Chloe Kelly, three Lionesses hungry to make their mark. What was so good about this squad was just how much talent they had – the players on the bench were just as strong as the starting eleven.

When the attendance was announced – 68,871 – the crowd roared again. Beth and the bench clapped too. *Wow!* A record for a Women's Euro game and it was only the first match!

At the final whistle, the players huddled together. Sarina would have to save her team talk for the dressing room – she had never heard a crowd as noisy as this before! Instead, the players joined the crowd to sing 'Sweet Caroline'.

Then it was time for interviews. The pitch-side journalists were keen to talk to the goalscorer. Beth was buzzing so much that she found it tricky to string a sentence together. The lights, the crowd, the music. . . What an amazing night it had been!

'It's beyond words,' Beth blurted into the mic. 'Our fans were incredible – they were our twelfth player!'

She was convinced they had helped suck the ball over the line for her goal! The most important goal of her life.

Interview over, Beth sprinted to find her family in the far stand. She desperately wanted to share this moment with her mum, dad and brother Ben. They had been her biggest supporters since the very start of her football journey. If you'd told six-year-old Bethany Mead that times like these lay ahead of her, she'd have likely screamed in delight.

Tougher tests would come, Beth knew that. But tonight felt as special as any night she'd known, and she was going to soak up every second.